Forty Poems

To Know the Meaning of Life

Muneeb Ahmed Qazi

ISBN 979-8589734607
Copyright © Muneeb Ahmed Qazi 2021
All rights reserved. No part of this book may be reproduced, or transmitted, in any form, or by any means (electronic, mechanical, photocopying, recording, or otherwise) without the prior written permission of the author.

Contents

Introduction 6

1. *The Search* 10
2. *Take a Break* 14
3. *The Question* 18
4. *Is there a Point?* 31
5. *No God? No Good!* 36
6. *Man and the Mannequin* 40
7. *True Happiness* 43
8. *From the Shackles Break Free* 47
9. *So What?* 52
10. *Way of the Wise* 55
11. *The Last One* 59
12. *The Trustworthy* 63
13. *Man and the Prophet* 65
14. *The Hills* 69

15. *The Prophet's Dates* 74
16. *The Prophet's Mercy* 77
17. *The Forbearing Forgiver* 80
18. *The Light* 84
19. *The Stream* 86
20. *The Intercessor* 89
21. *Why?* 93
22. *The Day of Recompense* 98
23. *The Promise* 102
24. *Be You Anywhere* 105
25. *Take Heed* 107
26. *The Impossible* 109
27. *The Veil* 112
28. *Beyond the Stars* 117
29. *Gardens of Heaven* 121
30. *Is it all Real?* 124
31. *O My Heart!* 127
32. *Tribulations Two* 130
33. *The Most Beloved Thing* 134
34. *The Prostration* 137

35. *The Last Bit* 139
36. *The Repentance* 142
37. *Am I Free?* 147
38. *Secrets of a Happy Life* 153
39. *One Step at a Time* 155
40. *Miles Away* 158
    Conclusion 161
    About the Author 164

Introduction

At some point in life, every human being asks himself a few common but very important existential questions. And it is okay to ask them. Who am I? What is the purpose of my life? What is life? Is there a meaning or purpose behind my life? And how did I end up on this planet? Was it all an accident, and is everything that I see just a random series of events that unfold before my eyes? Is there any meaning to any of this?

Philosophers, thinkers, and intellectuals have spent and continue to spend their lives trying to find the answers to these questions for themselves and for us. One of the most important questions inevitably tied to the aforementioned existential concerns is about the existence of God. No human civilisation flourished on this planet except that it grappled with this question of God.

Through these short poems, I attempt to answer some of these very questions. For some of you, this might sound a bit strange, especially for those who believe that the only way to know about anything is through science. In other words, the only way we can know about anything is when we can observe it with our senses or when we can conduct scientific experiments to establish it as fact. Empiricists generally hold such a worldview; and lately, empiricism has been gaining popularity, especially among the youth in the West, some of whom, by adopting this worldview, end up identifying themselves as agnostics or atheists.

Empiricism, if we were to call it a worldview, is a very unusual and impractical perspective for one to subscribe to. Even the proponents of empiricism in their actual lives do not and cannot fully implement the very worldview they so vehemently defend, for the biggest chunk of knowledge that we gain in our lives comes from testimony. It is impossible for us to conduct every scientific experiment that we read about before we really begin to believe in it or accept its conclusions. Furthermore, if any of our institutions, such as the judiciary or law enforcement agencies, were to adopt empiricism, they would collapse, as they largely rely on testimony.

Thus, it is not exceedingly difficult to see why empiricism is not an ideal, useful, or practical worldview to subscribe to in everyday life. Therefore, when it comes to finding answers to the ultimate questions of life, one should not heavily depend upon empiricism alone and should be open to other roots of knowledge such as testimony, logic, reason, or revelation.

And what if it was meant to be this way? What if we were meant to know God in this life by reason, logic, and revelation and not through empiricism and science? For at best, science can help us understand the 'how' questions. While it can explain how we and the things in our surroundings function, it can never answer why they function and exist in the first place. Science largely remains silent when it comes to the 'why' of things.

So, before we set off on this little journey to find answers to some of the existential questions we all commonly ask, I hope I was able to convince you (even if it was only a tiny little bit) that there are other roots to knowledge and that science is just one of many paths to knowledge.

The collection of these short poems is an attempt to understand and answer the existential questions we often ask ourselves. Many of them aim to point to the issues in our immediate lives that we face once we deny the existence of God, since the issue of God's existence is key to answering many of these existential questions. At the end of each poem is a brief summary that includes relevant information related to the poem to elaborate on what I meant to convey through the poems. The subjects of the poems are subtly connected to one another; therefore, they should be read sequentially. The use of masculine pronouns 'he', 'him', or 'his' is just for ease of language; the exclusion of female readers is not the intention.

Reading about abstract religious or philosophical topics can be a dull experience for some readers; therefore, I thought to make this an interesting experience by using beautiful poetic language, which people might enjoy reading, while keeping the poems loaded with information and sound philosophical ideas. Thus came about the idea of writing this book, which is now in your hands.

In my experience, being humble and open to ideas is key when it comes to understanding the issue of divinity. A person may be intelligent and well-educated, but arrogance may cause him to fail to see the truth. If you identify yourself as an agnostic or an atheist or even if you are a religious person, but somehow you doubt your faith, I encourage you to sincerely say what they call the 'atheist's prayer' before you begin.

'O God, if you are out there, please guide me.'

In my life, I have seen many people's lives change when they made an effort to seek God and to find the answers to the questions that troubled them for long. Out of desperation for the truth, many of them said one very special prayer at some point in their journey to find God. And almost all of them said remarkably similar words mentioned in the prayer above.

The Search

Went down another sun once again,
The one that ruled the heavens before this rain,
The hustle and the bustle of the city is gone,
Quite is the night, lifeless lay people in slumber again.

The light of the day has vanished,
The moon is now the new king,
Birds that once chirped went silent,
Crickets in the park now sing.

The streets lay deserted,
Who knows if they were ever full?
It is time to say goodbye again,
To this day that I lived so unmindful.

One by one the days come and go,
The nights orderly to the days follow,
And before I realise the path of my life,
A complete year forsakes me, abandons me and goes!

And yet there will come a day one day,
The morning of which will be the final one,
No sun for me will be waiting nor a new day,
No night for my resting will follow.

So let me take heed before that day,
Search for the meaning of this life and what follows,
Abandon my ways of ignorance,
Search for The Truth, to live by it and to follow.

Summary

Life is complicated. But one undeniable reality of this complicated life that we live is that it will one day come to an end. We will not be living this life forever.

At times we might get distracted and get caught up in the luxuries that surround our lives, so much so, that we might forget about this undeniable reality that awaits all of us. But what exactly happens after we die? Do we cease to exist? Do we all lose our consciousness once we die, and are we gone forever just like that!

And if we continue to live after we die, is there any relationship between this life that we live now, and our life after death?

These are very obvious questions one should not shy away from asking oneself and one must strive to find the answers for the same. In the pursuit of finding answers to these questions, one might ignorantly look for the answers in the wrong place and conclude that there aren't any answers. As is sadly the case with many empiricists, as mentioned in the introduction briefly, who by adopting empiricism deprive themselves of many legitimate paths to knowledge, like history or philosophy, and underestimate the many gifts we possess like reason, logic, intuition, or revelation, among others.

The first poem is aptly addressed to people who get distracted from asking these important questions we all should be asking, and to those who do ask these questions but look for their answers in the wrong place. Bit by bit, we will together try to find answers to these and many other such important questions, which I will be raising in the subsequent poems.

Take a Break

From the busy lives that you live,
Of studies, carriers, work and your bills,[1]
Take a break from it someday, sometime!
Take a breath, reflect, have some me time!

Is it all you would do in life, do think,
All your life you knew something was missing,[2]
What is it that you miss, reflect over it!
There is more to this life than money, love or your kids!

The more you think, the more you realise,
There is no meaning to your life without a divine,[3]
It is but a speck on the canvas of space,
Today you run, tomorrow there is no race!

In whichever direction you steer your life,
Know that death will end all of your strife,
Wake up from the slumber of your misleading works,
That which makes you forget your worth!

*To Him do you turn and ask for His help!*4
To show you your place in this deceptive web!
*Before you end up under this earth,*5
Without knowing who you were, and what was your worth!

Summary

1. We all get too busy and caught up in our lives. We spend our childhood enjoying ourselves in our innocent and childish games and plays, once we come of age, we find ourselves amidst loads of studies we need to do in order to find a decent job, once we find our jobs we worry about our promotions and some of us about marriage. Those who do get married and have kids find themselves worrying for their children, what they once used to worry for themselves! And amidst all this worrying, one hardly gets time to think about the very life one lives and the important questions that surround it.

2. But yet, deep down, people, however busy they might be, always find a void in their hearts that never quite seems to go. This void in their hearts makes them want to look for answers surrounding life and reality.

3. When people choose to reject God, all of a sudden everything around them including their own lives become meaningless or without any significance. There remains no meaning, value, or significance in their lives, or anything associated with their lives. There remains no purpose in life. Life becomes just a pointless accident that soon would come to an end.

Such people inevitably end up in depression and at times they come awfully close to taking their own lives, and many actually end up doing so. Therefore, it is essential for such people to question the conclusions they might have arrived at regarding the existence of God, which renders their lives to meaninglessness and depression.

4. A smart thing to do, would be, to ask God for His guidance, for if He really does exist, He would guide you and make you see the truth, and if He does not exist, you do not stand any chance of losing anything for a little private prayer that you secretly made for yourself! But on the other hand, if He does exist and there is an afterlife, and you die rejecting Him, it would not be that a great time, nor a place to realise the truth and meet the one who created you, having spent all your life rejecting Him and His signs, and His divine guidance of revelation.

5. This supplication to the Almighty along with a sincere investigation into the reality, meaning, and purpose of life should be given priority, and one should not end up procrastinating as life is too short, we only have a limited amount of time on this earth.

The Question

I gazed hard in the mirror to see,
A bright young boy staring back at me,
As if I never knew who he was,
The very first time me looking at me.

The eyes drew my attention the most,
Or was it my nose in between?
My ears stuck neatly by the sides,
My teeth kept peeping from within.

Both arms by my sides looked great,
So did my legs carrying my weight,
I kept staring at my body until,
A thought in my mind froze me all still!

Where was this body a billion years from now?[1]
Who is it that fashioned it so well and how?
The one who made it must be a magician,
I badly needed the story of my creation!

My parents could hardly assemble my toys,
Let alone create girls or some boys,
No answer I got could ever satisfy me,
Until my parents and teachers gave up on me!

This question remained even as I grew,
Until my children asked them anew,
So I set out one day to ask them again,
To scholars and scientists and all learned men!

'The body you got is 'cos you evolved,'[2]
A biologist told me, handsome and tall,
'It all started from a singular cell,
Resulting in all life, your question as well!

Your fight for survival got you here,
Mutation and selection gave you your ears,
Your bones, your flesh, your eyes and its tears,
There is no any creator, so brush away all your fears!'

'Are my eyes a result, do you try to suggest,
Given to me by a blind process?
My ears I use to hear you speak,
Chances of springing on their own seem so weak!'

'Do you not see all the evidence I cite?
Of genes, the fossils, ancestry and science,
Rejecting me you reject all science,
You seem no more than an ignorant in defiance!'

'The science you do is not absolute,[3]
Be it chemistry, biology or any of its offshoot!
Enough a theory I saw become redundant,[4]
The signs of a creator for me are abundant!

Even if I come from whatever you say,
How does it negate of what I have to say!
How does your theory reject a God?
Who could be behind this theory that you brought?[5]

The best you get to say is some life evolved,
No right you own to tell me of God,
Design is all I see wherever I turn,
My God is my designer I say in return!'

'Could you then try to explain?
Who designed this grand designer you claim?
Why is it that I do not ever see Him?
Or is He just made of your desires and your whims!'

'Silly is the question you pose,
His is the creation, He is the creator,
How can one create the uncreated?
Designed is the creation not the designer!

He is The First, He is The Last,
Originator of everything, the present, the future and the past,
He is The Eternal, The Almighty, The One,
Lord of the universe, The One and only One!

*Many a man I rejected who claimed He was three,
Those who made His idols of stick, stone or tree,
For me His oneness was crystal clear!
There is only one God one should fear!*

*On my journey to find Him I went through them all,
Many a scripture, books and metaphors,[6]
None for me could pass the test,
Save one altered and tampered were all the rest!*

*Quran[1] was the only scripture that could stand the test,[7]
Authentic, preserved, original, unlike the rest,
The one that argued for His oneness the most,[8]
Letting my heart at ease, and at complete rest!'*

---

[1] *Quran* is the word of God and the holy scripture of Islam.

Summary

1. The complex human body that we walk in and see every day in our mirrors, is probably the first sign of God we see every single day in our lives. This complex human body begs an explanation from every single one of us. How did it come about to be?

Was it all through the natural, random, and blind mechanism of natural selection, or was there any form of intelligence behind? Observing such complexities repeatedly in themselves and in nature, human beings have for a long time, and most of them even today, attributed it to a supernatural intelligent being, in other words, God.

2. This simple, largely accepted, observation and conclusion amongst people across space and time since the dawn of human civilisation began to get increasingly challenged in the late nineteenth century, as and when the theory of evolution started gaining attention and popularity, when Darwinists started attributing this complexity that we observe to evolution, rather than an intelligent supernatural being called God. People began getting attracted to this new explanation for the complexity that they observed in their daily lives, which did not require them to have faith in an unseen intelligent being,

who demanded their obedience and reverence at the cost of their own personal freedom, moreover, this new explanation was based on scientific observation and not merely on revelation and faith according to them.

3. People began putting all their eggs in the same basket of science, without considering a few very basic principles of the scientific method, upon which all philosophers of science agree. The most important one being that the scientific method never gives absolute truths due to the problem of induction. The same set of data, of any given observation can give completely different results with or without the addition of new data. So, like all the other scientific facts or theories, even the theory of evolution does not stand any chance of being absolute. Richard Dawkins, the famous populariser of this theory admits to this fact, and he says, 'We can now assert with confidence that the theory that the earth moves round the sun not only is right in our time but will be right in all future times even if flat earthism happens to become revived and universally accepted in some new dark age of human history. We cannot quite say that Darwinism is in the same unassailable class. Respectable opposition to it can still be mounted, and it can be seriously argued that the current high standing of Darwinism in educated minds may not last through all future generations. Darwin may be triumphant at the end of twentieth century, but we must acknowledge the

possibility that new facts may come to light which will force our successors of the twenty-first century to abandon Darwinism or modify it beyond recognition.'[2]

4. The history of science is filled with such examples, where a scientific fact held in consensus in the scientific community, was within a few decades regarded as obsolete, and a new scientific fact replaced the old. Take for example the steady state theory (according to which the universe was eternal), in the beginning of the twentieth century, there was a consensus amongst scientists that the steady state theory was a scientific fact, and just within a few years, after the discovery of the expansion of the universe by the Hubble telescope, this theory was discarded entirely by the same scientific community who previously claimed it to be an absolute scientific fact. This is not to say that science is somehow bad and unuseful. Science is one of the best tools in the hands of mankind, however, this tool that we possess has some limitations. And to reject divine revelation, which in essence claims to be absolute truth, by using this tool, keeping in mind its limitations and shortcomings, in all honesty, is disingenuous, inconsistent, and unwise.

5. Even if we agree for the sake of argument, that the theory of evolution is a fact and an eternal truth, in what capacity does it help the cause of atheism? The

---

[2] Dawkins, Richard, *A Devil's Chaplain: Reflections on Hope, Lies, Science, and Love* (Boston: Houghton Mifflin, 2003), p. 81.

theory of evolution only and only proves evolution, how does it prove the nonexistence of a creator God? A creator God can very well be behind evolution and its mechanism of natural selection. Therefore, jumping from the theory of evolution to conclude the nonexistence of God, and embracing atheism as a result, in many ways is akin to putting one's cart before the horse, and being intellectually dishonest and ingenuine at the same time.

6. We are back to square one, even if we accept the theory of evolution to be absolute, we still have no grounds to reject the existence of a creator God, the question of evolution's unexplained complex mechanism and all the complexities that we observe coming together on its own remains. How do we account for such breathtaking complexities we see in our lives, and everywhere else that we turn? Maybe the age-old natural human intuition, grounded in common sense, to ascribe it to a supernatural intelligence called God was true. But how do we know about this God? Whom should we trust, for there are many conflicting ideas around us regarding this God? Does this mean everybody is lying? Or is there someone who has the truth in this sea of conflicting ideas? Consider the following analogy to aptly deal with this dilemma.

Say you are lost in a forest, let us say you are lost in the biggest of them all, the Amazon Forest. You desperately want to find your way out; it is long since you ran out of your food and water. You tried your best to find your way out but to no avail. And just when you were about to give up, you see a few people. You get all pumped up and excited. They seem to look like tourists and outsiders just like you, and they say they are not lost. In fact, they know the way out of the forest. However, there is a little twist. None of these people agree as to which one is the right way out of the forest. Each one of them points in the opposite direction. Not only this, but they also claim their ways to be 'the only right way' and accuse each other of misguiding you. And just when you think things cannot get more complicated, you meet another individual who asks you to blindly choose any of the ways that you would like to, ultimately, they all take you outside the forest! What would you do in such a situation? You already tried your best to find your way out, and now you have a bunch of people who ask you to take opposite and conflicting directions in order to safely find your way out and save your life. What does one do in such a situation? Whom to trust? They all seem genuine, and you cannot just do nothing, for it is a life-and-death situation. And blindly accepting a random advice without much thought would imply that you are still lost, and that you for sure do not know your way out.

The most rational thing to do in such a situation would be to ask those people to present their best possible evidence to believe in them and take the path shown by them, instead of their counterparts. The person who presents the most convincing case, tells you what he saw on his way out of the forest, shows you some kind of a map as evidence, which does looks accurate and true, who seems genuine and honest and without any ulterior motives, should be listened to and trusted, in order to save yourself and attempt to safely find a way out of the forest. Because you cannot just give up and sit and do nothing, assuming that since they do not agree amongst themselves there is no way out, they all are lying. Because deep down you know there is a way out, the way through which you ended up there in the first place.

Such is the parable of life. We all are lost and look for answers when it comes to the ultimate questions of life. We cannot find these answers on our own, due to our very many limitations. All we have at our disposal, are a bunch of people or prophets who claim to know answers to these questions on account of them being revealed to them by God. We cannot reject them all at once, just because they do not agree with one another. The most rational thing to do would be to ask them to produce their best evidence for the claims that they make. So, in order to find answers to these ultimate questions, the least we could do is go through the revelations or scriptures these people or prophets claimed to have received from God, in other words, the best evidence that they possess.

When we study the major world religions like Christianity, Judaism, or Buddhism we come to know that many of them claim exclusivism, and denounce each other, while there are some which teach omnism, which basically means that all paths lead to God, and it does not matter which one you choose. Any student of comparative religion would know the logical impossibility of this claim. For there are irreconcilable differences among the major world religions and therefore all of them cannot be true at the same time. Christianity, or at least the majority of its denominations, revolve around the divinity of Jesus Christ, Islam calls Jesus Christ a man and its Prophet, and Judaism, on the other hand, rejects Jesus Christ completely altogether! To claim that all religions are the same and teach the same thing is often the result of being spiritually and intellectually lazy to be aware of these major irreconcilable differences among them.

Islam, however, has a very unique position, on one hand it claims exclusivism and to be the only way to reach God, but on the other hand, it recognises earlier faiths like Christianity and Judaism and acknowledges their divine origins. According to Islam religions prior to Islam and their prophets were inspired by the same God, but with the passage of time their teachings got corrupted and some even got lost, which eventually led to the very many differences we see among them today. Therefore, God sent His final prophet, the Prophet Muhammad with the last of His revelation, the Quran, to call people back to the same earlier teachings which got changed with the passage of time.

7. And since this was His last revelation, He took it upon Himself to preserve it till the end of times. When we, in all honesty, put all the world's religious scriptures to maybe, the most essential, even though not sufficient, test of preservation, only the Quran, according to both Muslim and non-Muslim scholars alike, passes this crucial test of preservation.[3]

8. If we reflect over just few of the many attributes of God we can philosophically construe, without the help of any religious scripture, like The Eternal (A created being creating the universe raises more questions than it answers. One might then ask who created this creator, leading one into the infinite regress fallacy), the All-Powerful (Think about the humongous number of atoms there might be out there in our universe, and the tremendous amount of energy stored in them all. This energy and more is at the disposal of the initiator of the universe i.e., God), the All-Knowing (Think about the meticulous fine-tuning of the universe, the intricate complexities we see within ourselves and around us and to initiate something like the universe, you sure need all the knowledge of the

---

[3] Tons of literature has been written on this topic. https://www.islamic-awareness.org is a good place to begin your research regarding this topic of preservation of the Quran.

universe and beyond), it becomes abundantly clear to us the logical impossibility of there being more than one God. No religious scripture on the face of this earth stresses upon the singularity of God as much as the Quran does. No page that you turn of it, but you find it affirming the oneness of God.

Is there a Point?

I see the world full of evils,
Is there really a point amidst all of these?
Rapes and murders, drugs and wars,
Death and destruction, poverty and disease!

There is a loving God people say,
Where is He when I witness all of these?
If He was so loving and All-Powerful,
He would have long stopped all this with ease!

Where was He when my loved one died?
Suffering from pain, a cureless disease,
With all the pain and sorrow that I had to go,
Could I ever say with me He is well pleased?

And yet there are millions and more,
Dying in floods, earthquakes, and tsunamis,
All along others who when meanwhile,
Die of hunger, thirst and poverty!

How many a crime would it take?
For Him to finally intervene,
Free this world from the evil clutches of man,
A so-called vicegerent unworthy!

I see no point behind all of this,
No wisdom behind a single thing,
I see a design in everything though,
The designer is nowhere to be seen!

This life that I go through gives me pain,
Why do I even believe?
The number of stories in His name that I hear,
Difficult it is to choose one, even if there's one truly His!

Why are there tyrant rulers?
And many a corrupt king?
Shedding blood of innocent men,
The very ones who put them in authorities!

Many a gangster, many a thief,
Take away people's lives and properties,
Why doesn't He ever stop this mess?
If He was truly The Almighty!

'O Son of Adam! how hasty you are!
In your judgement, works and deeds!
Life and death are not but a mere test,
To distinguish the unfaithful from my devotees!

I was right there when I took the soul,
The one whom you loved so dearly,
And for every pain that my faithful goes,
I keep for him ready a reward near me!

Death is but a time to end your test,
For a life to come that you don't see!
Where patience, faith, work and devotion are rewarded,
A world altogether different, that you now don't see!

And thus, do I test my servants,
With hunger and thirst, death and poverty,
The world and all that you see is but a test,
For a life of happiness and joy, bliss and peace of eternity!

So be you patient and take some heed!
For the day of justice guard your deeds!
The day when the righteous shall be rewarded,
Criminals on that day shall justly pay for their misdeeds![4]

---

[4] The messages given in the voice of God in this poem and the rest are all derived from the primary sources of the Islamic faith.

Summary

If you see this world in isolation of, and without considering an afterlife, the evil and suffering that takes place in this world, none of it makes any sense. But when you open your eyes and try to see the bigger picture and the life that is to come on the other side, which the revelation confirms, suddenly the world you see around you starts making more sense.

When we see people dying in disasters, natural or man-made, we get really moved and our emotions take over us, and we start to question the existence of God, due to the death and destruction that may take place before our eyes. We do so because our faith in God was weak in the first place. For if we were to have firm faith in God, we would not see death as the end of life and as a purely evil thing, we would see it as the beginning of a new life as promised to us by God.

In our hastiness we expect this life, and the world that we live in, to be filled with ultimate justice. We expect God to punish the wrongdoers and bring them to justice in this very world before our eyes, oftentimes, forgetting what God had said to us concerning them in revelation. Consequently, it is mentioned in the Quran,

'And never think that Allah[5] is unaware of what the wrongdoers do. He only delays them for a day when eyes will stare (in horror).'[6]

Thus, our weakness of faith in the promise of God becomes a cause for us to even begin to doubt the existence of God Himself!

One particular *hadith*[7] narration of the Prophet Muhammad recorded in *Sahih Al-Bukhari*, the most authoritative book in Islam after the Quran, completely changes one's perspective regarding the suffering one goes through in this life. It says that the Prophet said, 'No fatigue, no disease, no sorrow, no sadness, no hurt, no distress befalls a Muslim, even if it were the prick he receives from a thorn, but that, Allah expiates some of his sins for that.'

Therefore, the evil that we see around us is not evil in and of itself. Most of it that we see is the manifestation of the God-given free will that man exercises negatively, for which he shall surely be held accountable one day, the rest of it is a test for us or a punishment as a means to expiate our sins. And if we bear with it patiently both the test and the punishment, it only brings us closer to God and raises our ranks and purifies us for a life that is to come, a life of eternal bliss, in nearness to God.

---

[5] *Allah* is the Arabic word for God used by Muslims and Arabic speaking Jews and Christians alike.
[6] The Quran, Chapter 14, Verse 42.
[7] *Hadith* basically is the record of the traditions or sayings of Prophet Muhammad.

No God? No Good!

*I set out on a journey one fine day,
To know what in life was good,
To know it, cherish it and follow,
And to make my life all good.*

*'Follow your heart,' said one man,
'Follow it to know the truth,
Do whatever makes you happy,
Harm no soul and you will find all good!'*

*I did so until I ran into trouble again,
Following my heart was misguidance so plain,
Good for me was bad for the other,
Right for me was wrong for my brother!*

*For I met a man who said he is all good,
And he loved his animal like two spouses would,
He followed his heart and did what he did,
He hurt no soul he would often insist!*

Now how does one speak to an animal?
And know the harms of one's desires evil?
Following my heart was following deceit,
Far from over was my search for good indeed!

And so, I wandered in blind alleys,
Full of opinions, ideas and greed,
I searched for good everywhere,
No nook, no corner, I did spare!

Some said to me, 'Just follow the rules,'
'Never mind who gets them to choose,'
'Live your life as rest of us do live,'
'Break no law and you would have nothing to lose!'

To make up laws by oneself,
Impose on others to me made no sense,
Why make any laws anyway?
When there is no ground for them to stand and to stay?

For without a grounding these are just ideas,
Popping in different human heads,
There is no good, there is no evil,
If not for an All-Knowing Godhead!

The clouds of my confusion began to depart,
As I experienced an inspiration divine in my heart,
The only place where good was to be found,
Was in the commandments of the Lord, holy and sound!

Summary

Sometimes in our ignorance, we reject the idea of God just because we fail to make sense of the evil around us. But we fail to realise that once we reject God, we simultaneously reject the very cause which led us to reject God, that is evil itself. In the absence of God, good and evil get reduced to mere subjective ideas. The evil, despising which we abandon God does not remain evil anymore, and we lose any grounding for us to call the very same act evil anymore. It is the same case with good, good reduces to mere subjective opinion or feeling which can change from person to person.

People who deny God, in many cases end up adopting utilitarianism (which basically is the idea that espouses the greatest amount of good for the greatest number of people. In other words, as long as one's actions do not harm anyone and are not detrimental to society at large they can be acted upon. Pleasure should be preferred over pain) when it comes to ethics and morality or deciphering or choosing between a possibly good action over a bad one.

Utilitarianism, however, gives erroneous or flawed results, and sometimes it just does not work, as is alluded to in the poem, citing the example of people who practice bestiality. If a person is free to act and seek pleasure if he does not hurt anyone, how is one supposed to view the act of bestiality? On one hand, we have a human being who would, as abhorrent as it may sound, tell us that he finds pleasure in bestial relationships, but on the other, how can we ever find out whether the animal experiences pain or pleasure, or whether it even consents for such an act in the first place? Utilitarianism, which often is the refuge of people who deny God, for the most part just does not work. Bestiality, incest, pornography, and substance abuse are just some examples where utilitarianism simply fails to provide satisfactory answers.

Therefore, in the absence of divine commandments, the line between right and wrong blurs almost completely, and good and bad get reduced to mere personal subjective feelings or opinions of an individual. In the absence of God, there remains no real difference between the act of beheading an innocent child on one hand and saving one on the other, except that the latter would garner praise while the former would land one behind the bars.

Man and the Mannequin

Once a boy somewhere, sulked, cried and begged,
Until he made his father agree to buy him his favourite jacket red,
So off they went to the market to get,
This jacket which this young boy just couldn't forget!

And as he saw it displayed upon the mannequin,
The boy rushed to get it himself waiting for none,
And he had barely taken it off of it when,
The mannequin slipped and fell breaking in pieces ten!

'I killed the boy, I killed him!' the boy began to cry,
No words from his father to this boy could pacify!
To him he had turned into a murderer,
The moment the mannequin fell and broke due to his err.

'It had no life,' his father tried to explain,
'Lifeless it was to feel any pain,'
'Don't feel so bad we will make up for it,'
'Pay its owner what he owes us for it.'

'Is pain the only difference between us the human race?'
Asked the boy, as he began wiping his tears off of his innocent face,
'He had eyes and nose like me though he only stood still,'
'I thought he did so to sell his jacket out of his will.'

'What makes me different O father from a rock and a tree?'
'Besides that I feel pain and in the streets I roam free?'
'Why is it bad to be bad to a human?'
'Why is he valued more than anyone?'

Replied his father smiling, in his arms as he picked up his son,
'Were it not for The Almighty, The One,'
'There would be no real difference between man and a mannequin,'
'So blessed is He who blessed us and made us one amongst the humans!'

Summary

In the absence of God, we lose our right to differentiate ourselves and to ascribe value to ourselves from the inanimate objects or matter we see around us. There remains no special or real difference between a cup and the one holding the cup i.e., a human being. In the atheistic, materialistic type of worldview, there remains no real difference between the two, because, at the end of the day, both are just arrangements of matter of varying complexities. An innocent child falling from a building and dying is akin to a piece of glass falling down and shattering into pieces, there remains no explanation at all as to why both scenarios differ, or on what basis they differ if they really do differ.

On one hand we have this dark, unfathomable, depressing way of looking at things in the absence of God, on the other hand, we have the theistic way of looking at things, where we have value ascribed to life by the Life-Giver, we have morals, we have meaning, purpose, and reason to make sense of ourselves and our existence.

True Happiness

I looked for happiness in wealth and in possessions,
Rides beautiful and grand big mansions,
I thought I would be happy the more that I own,
But never stopped feeling lonely, on my own all alone!

I searched for it then, in love and in friends,
In every possible human relation,
Sons and daughters, parents and neighbours,
But this big void in my heart would never go.

I sought it by helping all those I could,
Feeding the hungry, standing for truth,
Nothing I did could ever fill up,
This void of my heart would always show up.

No tricks of distractions could ever help me,
The uneasiness inside me was for all to see,
Not much it took for me to begin to question,
The truth of this happiness which I sought so often!

What is the difference between pleasure and pain?
If in the end both are but chemicals of my brain?
Why would it matter which way I feel?
In the end if there is no meaning any real!

The errors of my ways I soon realised,
The meaninglessness of everything without a divine,
I now knew what in life I was missing,
The giver of my life and its meaning!

I now knew where my true happiness lied,
In remembering my Lord and following His guide,
Life and my actions without whom are all empty,
The giver of happiness, the Lord of all bounty!

Summary

No amount of worldly possessions can ever make a person happy. People mistakenly think that once they gain a certain amount of fame and popularity, or amass a certain amount of wealth, the problems of life would just go away, and they finally would be happy and achieve success. But this in fact is a deception. Countless cases of celebrities who end up committing suicide tell us a different story. These people own everything that an individual aspires to have in life, be it fame, popularity, wealth, family, or any worldly possession one could ever imagine. But yet, why do many of them still struggle with depression? And why do some of them end up taking their own lives? Canadian celebrity, Jim Carrey, regarding whom most of us would believe, that he 'made it big', or in other words achieved success, left everyone scratching their heads when he said, 'I think everybody should get rich and famous and (have) everything they ever dreamed of so they can see that that's not the answer.'[8]

So, what is the answer? What in life can make a person happy and give a feeling of fulfilment and contentment? What in life can give us a sense of peace, satisfaction, security, comfort, and achievement every night when we lay down ourselves to rest?

---

[8] Stone, Jay, "Of fun and fame." *The Gazette*, Montreal, 17 Dec. 2005, p. D13.

The Quran replies, 'Those who believe, and whose hearts find satisfaction in the remembrance of Allah, for without doubt in the remembrance of Allah do hearts find satisfaction.'[9]

The only place where we can find peace and satisfaction in this life is in the remembrance of God, and by fulfilling the God-given purpose of our life, which is to believe and acknowledge God and fulfil His injunctions upon us with sincerity, faith, and devotion.

---

[9] The Quran, Chapter 13, Verse 28.

From the Shackles Break Free

I am all free to do what I want,
Who could there be to question me?
Me my owner one and only,
No slave to none, no slave to no holy!

My decisions are mine,
Mine is my body,
No one to tell me right from wrong,
For I am completely free!

This was at least what I thought was true,
Until I had some realisation new,
I was in fact shackled and chained,
My claims of freedom were but bogus and vain!

For I thought of the billions who walk this earth,
How many of them were given a choice at their birth?
Who got to choose the colour of their skin?
Who got to choose two arms instead of two wings?

Who chose the land to walk upon?
To sleep at night or to wake up at dawn?
No choice there is in food nor in drink,
One can't even choose when not to blink!

You have the shackles of your desires you don't see,
Of people, society, friends and families,
Shackles of what others expect from you,
Chained up you are, and you never even knew!

Yet there is something which could truly set you free,
From these shackles help you break free!
When you submit to The One who created you,
You go from slavery to a freedom new!

Summary

If we just reflect for some time, we will realise that there is no such thing called as ultimate freedom, however much we would like to think there is. Just think about how much of a say we have on some of the very fundamental aspects of ourselves, which makes us who we are, and how we relate ourselves to others, and to the society at large. Did we get to choose the place or time of our birth? Did we choose our race? How about our sex? The colour of our skin? Who gets to choose whether they wish to eat food or abandon it completely just for a few days without losing life? Who got to choose the size and shape of the bodies that they walk in? We cannot even control the number of times we blink!

It is thus not exceedingly difficult to see why there is no such thing called ultimate freedom that we could enjoy. At times, we might think we are free, but in reality, we become slaves and submit to the prevailing and dominating ideas of our societies, without us even realising it. At times we become slaves to our biological desires, and at times to our greed and hunger for amassing worldly possessions. There is no individual who walks on the face of this earth who is free from worship and slavery, there are some who worship their carnal desires, others who worship money and fame, and some maybe the tradition or culture of their society that they were brought up in.

The message of Islam is quite simple. Abandon the worship of these false Gods, which could be your desires and whims, demigods, whom the society might have wrongly put up as equals to God, or it could be any other thing that you revere and follow, instead of the divine revelation and guidance given by God Himself through His Prophet. Consequently, God rhetorically asks in the Quran, **'Have you not seen the one who has chosen his desires as his Lord?'**[10]

Therefore, instead of submitting to one's desires or to the society or to anyone else it makes more sense to submit to one true God and follow His divine guidance, because in this life one can never achieve or even get close to achieving the ultimate freedom, there is no one except that he or she submits to something, the only difference is, it is either God and His divine guidance, or anything and everything else. Muhammad Iqbal, a famous Muslim philosopher, and poet from Pakistan alludes to just this beautifully, 'This one prostration (to God) which you deem too exacting liberates you from a thousand prostrations (to all others besides God).'[11]

---

[10] The Quran, Chapter 45, Verse 23.
[11] Cited in Riffat, H. (1968) *The Main Philosophical Idea in the Writings of Muhammad Iqbal (1877 – 1938),* Durham theses, Durham University. Available at: http://etheses.dur.ac.uk/7986/

At the onset, accepting God and an organised religion may seem like an infringement on an individual's freedom, but in reality, it liberates an individual from numerous chains and shackles which he walks in, oftentimes without even realising who and when put them upon his person.

So What?

So what if you walk seldom and often fly O man?
So what if your feet seldom touch the land?
So what if you own mansions majestic and grand?
So what if you have fleets of rides ready at hand?

You walk on earth with arrogance and pride,
No amount of pleas could ever stop your strides,
You walk past those dying of hunger and thirst,
You show arrogance and mockery to make it even worst!

You err O man you err indeed!
When you overlook those in need!
O you born weeping, weak and naked!
What on earth made you so boastful and wicked!

Is it the money which you think you made?
Or your sons who you think you did create?
Is it your mansions which you built to live?
Or the little strength of youth that He gives?

O you! O man! who when trip may die!
Your strength is not more than a fly!
Yet you walk on this earth a tyrant,
Transgressing, oppressing and defiant!

O you in deep slumber of arrogance!
Wake up before you wake with every sense!
As you die and know all that you did!
Restless, shameful, guilty, painful in utter mess!

Wake up! Recognise Him before it's too late!
Who created you with love and not hate!
Show Him that love and try to placate,
Your anger, your wrath, and your and unceasing hate!

So what if He is unseen?
Behold! He is closer than your very jugular vein!
Discover the joy in the discovery of The Supreme!
As your life turns from messed up to serene!

Summary

At times we get to falsely believe and delude ourselves that with money, wealth, and possessions that we own, we might be able to get away with any situation that we might come across in our life. This cannot be further from the truth. The variables that surround our lives are infinite, and in no way, shape, or form can we ever be in a position one day to gain control over them all. A small trip from one's staircase could result in one's death or the death of a loved one, and there is nothing we can ever do about it.

So where do we go from here once we realise this fragile reality of our existence? Do we just keep ignoring it and keep running away from it by distracting ourselves from this reality? Or do we finally accept that we are not in control of anything, not even our own lives, someone else is? The one who gave us our lives in the first place. Once we realise and give Him a place in our lives, the one who deserves it the most, that is our creator, once we open ourselves and humble ourselves to accept His divine guidance given to us in His final revelation, it only makes us morally and spiritually upright and works only for our betterment, we suddenly find our lives completely changed for our own benefit and for our own good.

Way of the Wise

'O God I know not how to live this life!
O God I know not if I could face this fight!
I know not if I am yet ready to face this challenge,
Life- which they blow as if it were a mere play!'

**'O Son of Adam! Get up and rise!
To lose hope is not at all wise!
Sure enough will thou find thy ups and thy downs!
But that doesn't justify to cease and to step down!'**

'O God I know not right from wrong,
That which shall harm me and destroy me all,
Teach me that from which I shall abstain,
Tell me wherein shall I be in great loss and wherein shall I gain!'

**'O Son of Adam! With thou shall thy God be well pleased,
If thou follow the one whom we have chosen among thee,
So follow our messenger sent for thou,
That thou know things to abstain from, and that which are allowed.'**

'O God Indeed thou are full of wisdom,
Knoweth everything open and hidden,
How could thou not send thy mighty men?
Without whom thy earth would have come to an utter end.'

Summary

'You have an excellent example in the Messenger of God; for anyone who seeks God and the Last Day and remembers God frequently.'[12]

A seeker of truth comes to a point in life where he realises and acknowledges the existence of a divine. But yet, his quest for the truth does not end here. How is he supposed to know more about this divine being in this life when He is unseen? What is the relationship with this being that he is supposed to have? How is he supposed to live his life, and from where can he get his moral codes for life? A beautiful conversation between this individual and the divine is captured in this poem. When this individual addresses the above-mentioned concerns, God refers him back to seek answers from the messengers He kept sending to guide mankind from time to time.

Muhammad, may peace and blessings of God be upon him, was one such individual who claimed prophethood, and affirmed the prophets who came prior to him. He is the only prophet in recorded history who affirmed all the earlier prophets of the Abrahamic faith, without which

---

[12] The Quran, Chapter 33, Verse 21.

the traditions of almost all the earlier prophets would have been a subject of great speculation and doubt. Muhammad, may peace and blessings of God be upon him, also had a remarkably interesting claim that none of the earlier prophets had. He claimed to be the last and final prophet and announced to the world that there would no longer be any prophets sent by God after him. Therefore, those who are seekers of truth cannot help but study and try to learn more about this individual who claimed to be the seal of the prophets and messengers sent by God. And in the upcoming section, we will try to do just that.

The Last One

On the hot and barren sands,
The desert of Arab lands,
Came the one who had to come,
Muhammad the Prophet, Muhammad the last one!

A seal of all those who had come,
Before him but with the message one,
That God of people is only one,
And that no son has He begotten!

But it was the way it was before,
Oppressed were the prophets sent before,
The fate of Muhammad was the same,
Like all his brothers he suffered the same!

The torture, the ridicule, and the pain,
Through it went all who brought this message same,
No prophet of God who said, 'He is one,'
They suffered all, the first and the last one!

'For thy Lord be patient,' God said,
'Continue to deliver what was aforesaid,
Until my message reaches the horizons,
And their first and their last receives my guidance.'

Toiled he, the Prophet, the blessed one!
Day in and day out with a message one!
'I am a Messenger; your God is one!'
'No prophet will warn you ever, for I am the last one!'

Fruits of his labour he began to see,
Waking up from their slumber as they began to see,
The truth of his message, the truth of his speech,
The light of the preacher, in what he preached!

Summary

Prophet Muhammad, peace and blessings of God be upon him, was born on a Monday, on the twentieth or twenty-second of April, 571 CE, in Mecca, present-day Saudi Arabia. He was born in a tribe called *Bani Hashim*. At the age of twenty-five, he worked for a lady merchant, by the name of Khadijah, who later on being impressed by the morals and conduct of the Prophet Muhammad, proposed to him for marriage, which he agreed to and eventually they got married. Khadija at the time of her marriage was forty years old, and she was the first woman Prophet Muhammad married. He did not marry to any other woman until she passed away.

Around the age of forty, Prophet Muhammad began to practice meditation in seclusion, in search of the Truth. He claimed prophethood around the same age and started calling people to what he claimed were revelations given to him by God. These revelations which he started to receive, continued for about a span of twenty-three years, which were later compiled into one codex or manuscript, known as the Quran, the primary and the most fundamental religious scripture of Islam.

This journey of calling people to God however was anything but easy. In the span of these twenty-three years, the Prophet Muhammad underwent massive tribulations and trials in his life, from the very people who honoured him prior to this new mission of his. Those who believed in him suffered the same fate. Despite all odds, Prophet Muhammad showed an unimaginable amount of resilience and faced all the hardships and difficulties that he had to face and did so until almost all of the Arabian Peninsula embraced this new faith in his lifetime before he passed away.

The Trustworthy

They sent for him the finest horsemen,
'Bring him back,' they said, 'dead or alive,'
Placed a bounty to allure all greedy men,
For they could not see his message thrive.

With all the hardship that he had to face,
In Mecca, his city, his beloved birthplace,
He knew soon he would have to leave,
His heart full of sorrow, pain and grief.

Among them he dwelt there all of his life,
To call it his home he took a great pride,
And here he was being driven out,
Oppressed and tortured, singled out.

And yet as he began to leave,
He asked to give away people's properties,
Entrusted to him by his very enemies, thirsty for his blood,
But he was the trustworthy, the noble, the Prophet Muhammad.

Summary

If you ever wish to ascertain the morals, conduct, and character of an individual, you should see how he treats his enemies. Here, we had a man being persecuted simply for professing and calling people to faith, attempts of assassinations being made against him, his followers being put to death before his eyes, but yet the Prophet, before migrating to Medina, due to the hardships that he had to face in his birth city of Mecca, did something which is very difficult for us to even imagine. He appointed his cousin, Ali Ibn Abi Talib, to return the properties that his enemies had entrusted with him, to their rightful owners. It is this unwavering quality of trustworthiness that the Prophet Muhammad had that earned him the title of *Al-Amin* (The Trustworthy) even before he began preaching the message of Islam.

Man and the Prophet

Travelled a man,
From distant a land,
To fight for the Prophet, to give him his hand,
In pledge of allegiance, to fight under his command.

Said he, 'I came to you from Yemen,'
'O Messenger of God sent unto all men,
Be thou be gracious and accept my pledge,
And make me one of thy company, the blessed!

I come to you to offer my support,
To this message of God, you brought forth,
Help me do jihad for this blessed cause,
To fight under your banner, the enemies of God!

I come to you leaving behind,
Parents old, who tried a lot in changing my mind,
Failing in which they couldn't help but weep,
For they are in their old age, vulnerable and weak!'

*'Do you come to me leaving them all alone?
Weeping and helpless, in their old age on their own?
Make them smile again, go back and serve them!
This is your jihad to enter the kingdom of heaven!'*

Summary

The word *jihad* is often the most misconstrued and misunderstood word, and oftentimes when people hear the word *jihad*, they think it simply means carrying explosives and blowing oneself up in some kind of a holy war!

This, however, cannot be further from the truth. The Arabic word *jihad* simply means to strive and to struggle. And yes this *jihad* can be done against one's enemies in a war, yes, in a war, because Islam is not a pacifist religion, it acknowledges the fact that people of two different geopolitical territories, different ideologies, different civilisations or based on any other differences might end up facing each other in the battlefields, forced by circumstances, so instead of ignoring this reality, it addresses it and lays down certain rules on how one should face one's enemies, if one has exhausted all the other options to peacefully resolve a pressing issue. And not every Muslim has the right to start this type of *jihad*, this type of *jihad* can only be initiated on the orders of a Muslim ruler, who when failing to resolve the given issue through peaceful means, and which if left unaddressed could pose a significant amount of threat to the territorial integrity of the Muslim land, its people or property, he can issue orders of *jihad* or in other words a war for a just cause.

But this is not the only meaning of *jihad*. *Jihad* can be of many different types. And the best type of *jihad* is to fight one's own evil inclinations and strive to try and become a better human being.

The poetised incident is recorded in *Sunan Abu Dawud*, where a man came to the Prophet covering a great distance, all the way from Yemen, and asked for his permission to take part in a military *jihad*. The Prophet asked him, 'Do you have parents?' The man replied in the affirmative and informed him about their disapproval of him leaving them alone. Upon hearing this the Prophet, may peace and blessings of God be upon him, ordered the man to return and to serve his parents well and said to him that this was his *jihad* for him.

The Hills

Up he went the hills in seclusion,
To pray and worship the Lord of all creations,
For days the Prophet would be in a cave all alone,
Looking for answers of the unseen and the unknown!

And one night came that changed it all,
When Archangel Gabriel descended and called,
'Recite O Muhammad,' he said,
'Recite I am the archangel whom God sent!'

'I know not how to read,' he muttered,
Terrified, aghast he could barely even utter,
The angel suddenly caught him and pressed,
Released him and said what he had aforesaid!

The reply of Prophet was the same,
I am unlettered was his only claim,
The angel then caught him again,
Released him and thus the revelation began!

**'Recite in the name of thy Lord who created,
Man, from a clinging clot He created,'**
*Receiving this revelation, the Prophet descended,
His heart beat profusely, to his home as he hurriedly headed!*

*'Cover me up, cover me up,' he cried,
Narrated all of what happened to his wife,
He thought he had almost lost his life,
Were it not for the faith of his faithful wife!*

*'Never will God disgrace you,' said she,
'In His name you help the poor and needy,
Ties of the kith and kin you keep,
With generosity to one and all you treat!'*

*'Soon will they drive him out,' said a learned man,
'Fight the Prophet's message with all that they can,
How I wish I live to see that day!
To support God's message, and to fight for His way!'*

Summary

The name of the angel who brought the revelation to Prophet Muhammad was Gabriel. The mere word *angel* does not sit quite well when it falls on the agnostic or atheistic ears. 'Do you still believe in angels?' 'Grow up!' These are the quite common reactions and responses one gets to hear upon just mentioning this word.

However, when you really think about it, when an individual recognises the existence of God and sees himself and everything around as God's creation, it is not very difficult to imagine that God could create a different creation called angels which we fail to see, just as we fail to see God with our eyes in this life. Belief in angels is one of the six pillars of faith in the religion of Islam.

Prophet Muhammad, peace and blessings of God be upon him, as mentioned previously would meditate for long hours in isolation, in a cave called *Hira*, located in Mecca, present-day Saudi Arabia. After a span of some period of time, his long meditations to seek the truth bore him fruits. One special night, in the month of *Ramadan*,[13] he received his first revelation.

---

[13] *Ramadan* is the ninth lunar Islamic month in which Muslims fast during the daylight hours.

> 'Recite in the name of thy Lord who created,
> Man, from a clinging clot, He created,
> Recite and thy Lord is Most Generous,
> Who taught by the pen,
> That which knew not the men.'[14]

Thus, at the age of forty years, Muhammad may peace and blessings of God be upon him, was honoured by God with prophethood. The initial reaction of Prophet Muhammad was horror and shock, and he was frightened by this encounter to his core. It was at this moment of great crisis in his blessed life that his wife Khadija stood by him, supported him, and believed in him when no one else believed. On the night when this incident of first revelation happened, when Prophet Muhammad encountered the angel near the cave for the first time in his life, he got frightened as anybody else would have, so he rushed to his home where his wife comforted him. And after he narrated to her what had happened, she reminded him of his virtuous deeds and character and said that God would not let them go in vain and would not leave him unassisted. She then took the Prophet to her cousin, Waraqa Ibn Naufal, who was a Christian, familiar with the gospels. And upon hearing the story of his nephew, he said,

'I wish I were young, and I could live up to the time when your people will drive you out.'

---

[14] The Quran, Chapter 96, Verses 1 to 5.

'Will they drive me out?'

'Yes, anyone who came with something like what you brought today except that he was treated with hostility, and if I should remain alive till that day when they drive you out then surely, I will be one of your strongest supporters.'

However, Waraqa Ibn Naufal died shortly after this incident and the divine inspiration stopped for a while.

The Prophet's Dates

It was the month of Ramadan,
When in the service of the Prophet came a man,
'I broke my fast O Prophet,' said he,
'O Messenger of God! do thou guide me.'

'Go ye! your Lord is forgiving,
He forgives man's every sin,
To expiate your sin go free a slave,
Such is the command which your Lord gave.'

'O Messenger of God! I am weak,
In all honesty to you do I speak,
To free a slave for me is impossible,
Over your command you do mull!'

'Go ye! seek His forgiveness,
For your misdeed you fast for two months,
Indeed your Lord is Most Forgiving,
Such is the command of your Lord which I bring.'

'O Messenger of God! I am weak,
Fasts of Ramadan I could not complete,
Fasting for two months for me is heavy,
So gracious be thou to my plea!'

'Go ye! your Lord sees and listens,
In His path you feed sixty men,
Indeed your lord is Most Forgiving,
Such is the command of your Lord which I bring.'

'O Messenger of God! I am weak,
To feed sixty men is beyond my reach,
Be thou be gracious upon me,
O Messenger of God! do thou guide me!'

'Go ye! take these dates from me,
Give ye to the poor and the needy,
Indeed your Lord is Oft-Forgiving,
Upon His slaves He showers His blessings.'

'O Messenger of God! indeed I am poor,
No poor of Medina from me can be poor,
So be thou be gracious upon a poor man,
Give him out of your bounty what you can!'

A smile broke across the Prophet's blessed face,
As he hearkened to the man with utmost grace,
'Go ye! and take all of these,
Eat my dates until ye are pleased.'

Summary

The poetised incident is recorded in *Sahih Al-Bukhari*. A man came to the Prophet, may peace and blessings of God be upon him, completely crestfallen and dejected sometime in or around *Ramadan*, the month in which Muslims observe fasting during the daylight hours. *Ramadan* holds a great significance in Islam, as it was the month in which the revelation of the Quran began, this further added to this man's disappointment over his sin of breaking his fast by engaging in intimate relations with his wife, which along with food and water and some other things breaks a person's fast. Feeling guilty about what he had done, he came to the Prophet to ask about the expiation for his sin and the means to achieve it, and thus the conversation poetised in this poem took place between this man and the Prophet.

The Prophet's Mercy

The light from the heavens that he received,
He wished to share it with all those in need,
But they chose their darkness over this new light,
Mocked him the Prophet and crossed every height.

He thought maybe the others would see this truth,
People of another city, its old and its youth,
So off he went to Taif, having high hopes,
Never knowing ever, that it would be but a slippery slope.

For instead of seeing this light and this truth,
They pelted on him stones, many a wicked youth,
They pelted him with stones until he bled,
With the hot desert sun shining over his head.

The blood from his wounds began to trickle down,
Collecting in his shoe as it fell to the ground,
Until his blessed shoe got stuck to his feet,
Under the desert sun's scorching hot heat.

Drenched in blood when he sat on the ground,
Taking shelter in a place safe that he had found,
Two angels in his presence appeared just then,
Sought his permission for a just revenge.

His compassion and mercy for the wicked became a shield,
Even when his wounds were still fresh and unhealed,
Forgiving them all who almost killed him he said,
Maybe their progeny will believe in him instead.

Summary

This heart-wrenching incident occurred in the tenth year of the prophethood towards the end of May or the beginning of June in 619 CE. Taif, which is located at a distance of about 60 kilometres from Mecca, got the attention of Prophet Muhammad for conveying the message of Islam, after facing very many challenges in Mecca. He expected a different response in a new city, contrary to that of hostility that he received from the people of Mecca. Despite trying his best to convey this message of God, for ten days straight in the best of possible ways, the people of Taif took to violence and pelted the Prophet with stones until he began to profusely bleed. And when he was presented with an option of just revenge by the angels, he, may peace and blessings of God be upon him, chose forgiveness and said, 'No, I hope that Allah will let them beget children who will worship Allah alone and none besides Him.'[15]

---

[15] Narrated by Bukhari. The *hadith* are referenced by their compilers. Narrated by Bukhari means that it is in the *hadith* book compiled by Bukhari.

The Forbearing Forgiver

On his way he was with ten thousand men,
To his beloved city out from which he was driven,
For a decade its dwellers did torture him,
No man that stood for support but suffered with him.

Believers in the Prophet would be chained,
Locked up, killed, butchered and maimed,
Belief in one God was their only crime,
And acknowledging the Prophet of their time.

Sons who believed were shunned by their fathers,
Slaves who believed got slayed by their masters,
Women and children met the same fate,
For a decade they remained all victims of hate.

The army of Muhammad was today to enter the gates,
People of Mecca were certain of a death that awaits,
For they knew what they did to him in the past,
In horror they stood, terrified and aghast.

But he was Muhammad, the forbearing forgiver,
Who did something that was not done ever,
He forgave them all the first and the last,
Took one city like none did in the past.

Summary

For over a decade, the people of Mecca tortured Prophet Muhammad and his followers simply for professing their faith in one God, which eventually led to their migration to the city of Medina. The polytheists however did not desist from fighting the Prophet even after his migration, until they entered into a very famous peace treaty in the Islamic history, known as the *Treaty of Hudaibiya*. This treaty brought a significant amount of calm and simmered down the tensions and hostility between the polytheists of Mecca and the Prophet Muhammad and his followers in Medina to a certain extent for some time. However, it was unilaterally broken by the pagans of Mecca which prompted the Prophet Muhammad to withdraw from this treaty and finally set out to conquer the city from which he was expelled almost a decade ago.

Every other person in this army of Muhammad, who set out to conquer the city of Mecca suffered directly or indirectly at the hands of the people of Mecca, in the most brutal of ways imaginable, a huge brunt of it was meted out to the Prophet himself, not for a few days or a couple of years, but for almost over a decade. If any person at that time had any right for just revenge, it was

Prophet Muhammad. Being the person that he was, he chose forgiveness over revenge, love over hate, peace over violence, death, and destruction. He forgave the Meccans wholesale, the first one of them and the last, and set an example for the world to see and follow. And thus, he conquered the city of Mecca in the most peaceful of ways, without any bloodshed or violence, the likes of which was never seen in the recorded human history aforetime.

The Light

On coldest of cold nights,
Up he would be to receive the light,
The light of guidance from the heavens,
Upon his heart slowly as it would descend.

The descendance of it would be heavy,
Enormous, magnanimous and mighty,
Pain it was with which he received it,
The words of the Most High, bit by a bit.

Drenched in sweat on coldest of nights,
For it was not too easy to handle the light,
Yet the Prophet of God went through it all,
To see the way, and to show it to us all.

The humble saw it and those willing to see,
For the light was pure, divine and free,
The arrogant however chose to neglect it,
Fought the message and those who did accept it.

Summary

Narrated Aisha (the mother of the faithful believers), 'Allah's Messenger was asked, "O Allah's Messenger, how does the revelation come to you?" Allah's Messenger replied, "Sometimes it is revealed to me like the ringing of a bell, which is the hardest upon me, and sometimes the angel comes in the form of a man and talks to me, and I grasp whatever he says."' Aisha added, 'Verily, I saw the Prophet while the revelation was descending upon him, on an extremely cold day. Then it ceased, and his forehead was flooded with sweat.'[16]

---

[16] Narrated by Tirmidhi.

The Stream

He was Muhammad, to follow him is one's pride,
He was Muhammad, a Prophet, a guide,
Guide to the path of God, a light shining bright,
From depths of darkness, he showed the path to a new light!

He was Muhammad, who strove hard every day of his life,
Loved those whose hearts with hate for him were rife,
He was Muhammad to whom were given the keys,
To make people see what they did not see!

He was Muhammad, to whom God gave His words,
And showed all the way, to the Lord of the worlds,
Made him a guide, gave all the news,
Of gardens and rivers through it that ooze!

He was Muhammad the gentle, the forgiving Prophet,
The one who even forgave those who killed his beloved,
He was Muhammad, the brave warrior of God,
Who fought many a battle for truth and for God!

He was Muhammad the kind, who taught one to love,
Neighbours as brothers and the Lord Most High above,
He was Muhammad the just, who taught justice,
Even against oneself, friends or families.

He was Muhammad the prince, the bringer of peace,
Who united the people under the banner of tawheed,[17]
He was Muhammad, mankind's pride and esteem,
May my Lord grant me a drink from his beautiful stream!

---

[17] The word *tawheed* is used to refer to the oneness of God in Islam.

Summary

In heaven, there exists a stream by the name of *Al-Kauthar*. Prophet Muhammad often used to mention this stream to his companions. He foretold that on that day of judgement his followers would gather near this stream and many of his fortunate followers would be served water from this stream by the Prophet himself, after which they would never feel thirsty ever again.

When people who deny God are told about the afterlife, their reaction is that of outright disbelief. But if one really thinks about it, if this life is possible, why an afterlife is not? If you think about the odds against which the universe is finely tuned to the life-permitting range, by observing the fundamental constants and quantities of the universe, you will hardly doubt the possibility of an afterlife.

But, as for the people who recognise the signs of God they see all around them, and firmly believe in the existence of God, for them believing in an afterlife is fairly simple, if God can create them out of nothing and give them the life which they live now, why can't He assemble their bones and give them life for a second time?

The Intercessor

*The stars from the heavens rain down,
Joint together are the sun and moon,
Mountains are dust, the earth levelled,
Not a soul that once walked but is in swoon!*

*One by one they split the earth,
And from every grave they rise,
They rise for a day they thought would never come,
But the day of reckoning was long due!*

*They gather all the first and the last,
Each and every soul in a body new,
'Who is it that raised us all?' they ask,
'To this world so different, so new!'*

*The court of the Mighty will soon begin,
Anxious are all sinners, fearful,
Helter-skelter they run for help,
Only if they prepared for this day which was long due!*

Adam denied to help outright,
So did all prophets who followed suit,
'My soul, my soul,' they all cried,
'No help there is we can offer you!'

And as the time for judgement drew closer,
God's mercy being their only refuge,
The eyes of sinners begin to sparkle,
As they see Muhammad lying in sujood.[18]

'Rise, O Muhammad!
Raise up your head!
Ask, O Muhammad!
You ask today, you get.'

'My people, My people!'
'My people' is all he will say,
With choked voice, teary eyes,
As he lifts from the ground his blessed forehead.

And one by one your Lord will free,
The direction his blessed finger be,
The joy of sinners will know no bounds,
From hellfire as they begin to set free!

---

[18] *Sujood* is an Arabic word which means prostration.

Summary

The poem captures the fear, anxiety, and hope of forgiveness the believing sinners will have on the day of judgement. Though they believed in the message of God that their Prophet brought to them, they fell into temptation and gave into sin in the worldly life. Such people will have two hopes on the day of judgement. The first being in the divine mercy of God and His forgiveness, and the second in the intercession of the Prophet Muhammad.

Consequently, Abu Huraira narrated, 'We were in the company of the Prophet at a banquet, and a cooked (mutton) forearm was set before him, and he used to like it. He ate a morsel of it and said, "I will be the chief of all the people on the day of resurrection. Do you know how Allah will gather all the people, the first and the last in one level place where an observer will be able to see all of them, and they will be able to hear the announcer and the sun will come near to them? Some will say, 'Don't you see in what condition you are and the state to which you have reached? Why don't you look for a person who can intercede for you with your Lord?' Some people will say, 'Appeal to your father Adam.' They will go to him and say, 'O Adam! You are the father of all mankind and Allah created you with His own hands, and ordered the angels to prostrate to you and made you live in paradise, will you not intercede for us with your Lord? Don't you see in what miserable state we are in, and to what condition we have reached?' On that, Adam will reply, 'My Lord is so angry as He has never been before and will never be in the future. He forbade me to eat from the tree, but I disobeyed Him. (I am worried about) Myself! Myself! Go to somebody else, go to Noah.' They will go to Noah and say, 'O Noah! You are the first amongst the Messengers of Allah to the people of the earth, and Allah named you a thankful slave, don't you see in what state we are and what condition we have reached? Will you not intercede for us with your Lord?' Noah will reply, 'Today my Lord has become so angry as He had never been before and will never be in the future. Myself! Myself! Go to Prophet (Muhammad).' The people will come to me, and I will prostrate myself underneath Allah's throne. Then I will be addressed, 'O Muhammad! Raise your head! Intercede, for your intercession will be accepted and ask, for you will be given.'"[19]

---

[19] Narrated by Bukhari.

Why?

Why to wake up, why get up from my bed?
Why to earn when I have my bread?
What to learn, how long and why?
It all seems a mess, why even give it a try?

Why to make right what is wrong?
Whose right to take, and leave whose wrong?
Why to own when I will lose it all in the end?
Why to put up a smile when I know I just pretend?

Why prefer pleasure over my pain?
When in the end both are the same?
Why to be happy, and not to cry?
Why to speak the truth, and not to lie?

Why be honest to toil and sweat?
When one can get it easy, without any regret?
Is there really a point to any of this?
The world and everything that there is!

The more I think the more I realise,
There is no meaning to my life without a divine,
Pointless my life is without Him, The One,
To Him whom every soul shall return!

Summary

'Why' is such an important question we need to ask ourselves in life. Why live life? Why do what we do? Say an individual has enough money to last for his lifetime, has a family, a comfortable house to live in, fame, power, and popularity, and whatever worldly possession one could ever imagine, what purpose or goal then remains for such a person to pursue for the rest of his life?

The little goals that we might set for ourselves in life, like graduation, a nice job with a decent amount of money, a nice house, starting a family, or maybe some business, all of this might keep us busy for a while from asking the 'why' question, but once we achieve our self-given goals, the 'why' question never leaves us no matter how hard one tries to ignore it by indulging in a hedonistic or pleasure-seeking lifestyle. This 'why' question would never stop following us wherever we go in life.

So, what is the way forward? Are there any answers to these questions? Why live life if one does not enjoy it and did not get to choose it in the first place? Why do good and what is good? What is the purpose of life? When it comes to these types of ultimate questions science does not offer any help. Science remains silent when it comes to the 'why' of things.

Imagine asking these types of questions, and the answers that are out there in the garb of science.

'Why should I live? What is the purpose of my life?'

'Survival and reproduction. The greatest rationale is the propagation of one's genes.'

'But I do not like to survive, as life is full of pain! Nor do I want to reproduce. I simply hate life…. even more so, I hate having kids!'

What kind of scientific experiment could ever motivate such an individual, or any individual for that matter, to live a healthy, happy, and fulfilling life? The truth is, when it comes to these types of ultimate questions, science is not the right place to look for the answers. The only one who could answer such questions is the one who gave us our lives in the first place. And He did so in His final revelation, the Quran.

Our lives and our existence only make any sense when we acknowledge God and the life that He has promised us after death. When we look at this world in isolation from the hereafter, this world and everything in it is rendered to meaninglessness. What could possibly explain the death of some innocent child in an accident if one rejects God and an afterlife? All the finest doctors in the world would very well explain the causes and the injuries that led to the child's death. But could anyone ever explain why he met with this accident at such an early age in the first place? Why did he not get a chance to experience more in life like others or why did he die at this point in time and not a natural death later when he gets old?

In the absence of God and an afterlife, the realities and events that surround our lives get reduced to nothing more than a rearrangement of matter.

Therefore, belief in God and the revelation given to the Prophet Muhammad which informs us about the afterlife, if it does anything, it adds meaning to life and answers the ultimate questions that surround our lives, just as the existence of God adds meaning to morality and ethics, the afterlife adds meaning to the finite lives that we experience before death.

The Day of Recompense

The day of recompense fast approaches,
The day when all the wrongs will be undone,
The day when all oppressors would wish,
Would that we never did what we had done!

The day when no possessions would avail,
No son, no friend and no brother,
'Myself, myself,' will all cry,
'This day no one can help the other!'

In no profit will that day be the deniers,
Who denied the coming of this day in truth,
All the deeds they did would go in vain,
Who covered in falsehood the evident and the truth!

Take heed O man before it's late!
Over your actions you do contemplate,
Give up your arrogance and try to placate,
Your anger, your desires, your unceasing hate!

*Believers that day shall be received,
In honour and dignity, no fear, no grief,
Content with what their Lord gives,
Gardens with rivers flowing from beneath!*

Summary

The religion of Islam has six pillars of faith: belief in one God, belief in God's messengers (Muhammad being the final one), belief in angels, belief in God's revelations, belief in the last day (i.e. day of judgement), and belief in the divine decree.

If there is any pillar of faith after the belief in one God and His Messenger that is most often stressed in the religion of Islam and its literature, it is the belief in the last day i.e. the judgement day.

Belief in the last day, the day of ultimate justice and recompense helps a believer tremendously to make sense of the world and the events that take place in his life or surrounding it. People who forget this promise of God that He makes in His scripture, the promise of ultimate justice and accountability, the promise of reward and punishment, when such people encounter injustice or some form of suffering, they end up questioning the existence of God Himself, and further themselves even astray and away from the reality and truth. On the other hand, some people who do good, when they fail to see the fruits of the good that they do in this life, end up in the same position.

Believers, however, who have firm faith in God and in the Last Day, remain grounded in every situation that they might face in life in favour or against them. For they honestly believe in God and His promise of ultimate justice in the afterlife and that God would never bring their good works and patience to naught.

The Promise

Come in my way all the troubles that may,
Hardships, difficulties, endless roadblocks all my way,
I must never give up, I must continue,
For my Lord is Truth, His promise is true.

Even if I fall a thousandth of time,
They laugh at my failure, it all looks a steep climb,
I must rise up, I must continue,
For my Lord is Truth, His promise is true.

It may look at times life is but pain,
Unfair, unworthy, full of complains,
I must still go on, I must continue,
For my Lord is Truth, His promise is true.

And at times when I mess up beyond repair,
Be almost certain I could no longer bear,
I must put in Him all of my hope,
Trust His plans, clinch harder His divine rope!

And I must do this until I see,
Light, at the end of the tunnel where all darkness flees,
Fruits of my patience will I count then,
When my journey to the hereafter begins!

Summary

Having faith, as easy or abstract as it may sound, can at times be the toughest thing to do in a person's life. For this life and this world was meant to be this way, a test for a life of eternity to come after death. Consequently, the Quran mentions, **'And we will surely test you, with something of fear and hunger, and loss of wealth and lives and fruits, but give good tidings to the patient. Who, when disaster strikes them say, "Indeed we belong to Allah and indeed to Him we will return." Those are the ones upon whom are blessings from their Lord and mercy, and it is those who are the (rightly) guided.'**[20]

Therefore, when life gets tough, we get ridiculed for our faith, and face difficulties for having faith, we must never give up, we must put our trust in God and know that His promise is true. We must know that in the end, it is the believers who would rejoice.

---

[20] The Quran, Chapter 2, Verses 155 to 157.

Be You Anywhere

Be you in any corner of the earth,
On top of mountains, or in furthest of deserts,
Be you in the most distant of lands,
But know that your death and your life both are in His hands!

Black and the white, weak and the ones with might,
Peasants and servants, masters and merchants,
Oppressed and oppressors, wronged and wrong doers,
He will gather you all! no matter where you are!

Be you in the best of your health,
Or down with a disease lying on a bed,
Be you in your youth, or as old as one could,
Remember one and all! He will gather us all!

That day shall one pay in full,
For the deeds that one does today unmindful,
So beware of that day and take some heed,
And give up for this temporal world some of your greed!

Summary

Even after the dawn of the realisation of God's existence and an afterlife, a person might end up procrastinating to act upon this new realisation. The reasons could be many, and of the many, greed for this material world and its pleasures should never be underestimated. Because this greed for what is in front of us today might lead us into delaying to take this new path of realisation, the path of God, and at times it may even leave us completely deprived of it.

Therefore, it is incumbent upon us to set our priorities straight. No doubt benefiting from this material world in legal ways is completely acceptable in Islam, for Islam does not espouse any form of ascetic life in isolation from all worldly matters. However, what it does say is to strike a balance between this world and the next. Love of this world should not come at the cost of eternal salvation, nor faith and religious deeds a person does for the afterlife should become a hindrance to the worldly life and fulfilling one's worldly obligations and responsibilities.

Take Heed

Take heed before that day comes,
When children by their mothers get abandoned,
Friends that day shall turn into foes,
No one shall that day be, but in woes!

The day when mankind will be gathered again,
When this world we live in comes to an end,
The day of judgement, the day of horror,
The day when a brother would abandon his brother!

No money that day will come to any aid,
No barter, no compensation, nor trade,
Each soul that day shall be in grief,
Except the people of good deeds and belief!

People who believed in their Lord,
Worked for His pleasure, an eternal reward,
Their Lord with them that day would be well content,
As He rewards them for their struggles that they underwent!

Summary

To achieve the material wealth of this temporal world we toil and work with determination and channel our efforts in the right direction. We never complain about the efforts we have to put in for it, for we know that there is no gain without pain. So then, how could we expect for ourselves a life of eternal bliss, comfort, and salvation without putting in any effort and working towards achieving this tremendous goal?

The currency that we earn in this world by our hard work does not work in the hereafter or the next life. For the only currency of the hereafter is faith and righteous deeds that we do in this life. The more of this currency that we possess on the day of judgement, the chances of our salvation will be the more.

The Impossible

They say it is impossible,
Never will we be raised up again,
There is no heaven, nor any hell,
Nothing it is, but misguidance so plain!

How many generations have died before?
None came to life at all!
It is but myths and legends,
Deluded are believers, that's all!

For when we see not a thing,
We reject it and refuse to believe,
Why should we trust a mere mortal like us?
Who calls us to have faith, who calls us to believe!

See not the ones who say so, the life that they have?
From where did it come to be?
If from dirt and from dust you have what you have,
Why then is another life impossible to be?

Know that He will raise you, the first and the last,
Show you what you did in the life of your past,
Admit in His mercy those who strived in His path,
While His rejectors that day would earn nothing but His wrath!

Summary

When we reflect deeply on the realities that surround us, the life that we live, the food that we eat, the rain that descends from the heavens, the vegetation that grows therewith, and the beautiful celestial bodies swimming in the skies, it is not exceedingly difficult to see why many philosophers who deny God end up denying reality itself! They end up doubting their own existence and what their eyes see, for the reality that surrounds us is nothing short of a miracle, and it is very difficult to believe in miracles at times!

People who reject God end up rejecting this life that they experience and equate it to some kind of delusion, no doubt such people find believing in an afterlife, which they have not even experienced yet incredibly challenging and difficult.

Believers on the other hand, who recognise God's signs in and around themselves, remain firmly grounded in this life. For them, it is pretty easy. If this life is possible why not is the next? If a creator God can create them once, why not a second time?

The Veil

The Lord Most High took a veil of light,
Magnificent, magnanimous, splendid and bright,
That which prevents His creation to see,
The face of His Majesty, Nobility and Might!

And He did so out of His divine mercy,
That which allows His creation to exist and to be,
For if He were for a while to take off His veil,
All creation would tremble, destruction would prevail!

And to look at His face is a bounty so great,
Not every soul has this wondrous fate,
A blessing as such for which one has to work hard,
Believe in Him, worship Him and keep His commands.

For such faithful and pious will come a day,
That for which they long, and earnestly pray,
A day on which they will set on Him their eyes,
A day when they will enter His paradise!

Summary

People often say, 'We will believe in it when we see it,' or that, 'Science teaches us to ask and to learn, whereas religion teaches us to merely believe.' This, however, cannot be further from the truth. No person walks on this earth except that he has faith. In fact, without faith, not a single human being would be able to function in any way, shape, or form.

In order to even begin practising science a person needs to have faith. Faith, that the world that he observes to practise science is in fact real and not some kind of illusion. Faith that his senses that are to be used in the process i.e., the sight, the hearing, or that of the touch are in fact reliable and are truth-oriented, as such to produce results that correspond to the reality and the world outside.

No person who walks on this earth can walk without believing that he is a real person and not some illusion. And those people who do really end up doubting themselves, are the ones who doubt the existence of God. For God says in the Quran, **'And be not like those who forgot Allah, so He made them forget themselves, those are the defiantly disobedient.'**[21]

---
[21] The Quran, Chapter 59, Verse 19.

The truth is, there is no escape from faith in this life. The only difference is that the faith that we might have may either correspond with reality or at times it simply may not. Therefore, we all need to scrutinise our beliefs and our faith and try as hard as we can to align it with reality.

The question, however, is, why is it that we must have faith? Why is it not possible to not have any faith? Well, the answer is fairly simple. It is because of the fact that we are contingent, finite, limited, created beings with a beginning. Say, if we were all to see God with our own eyes in this life, and hear Him say what He wants from us, for securing our place in His paradise, won't we still need faith to believe that God, the being that speaks to us, is in fact the one who created us? And how would we even know that this being who speaks to us is in fact who he says he is, and not some evil alien trying to trick us? How are we supposed to witness the beginning of our own creation when we at that point in time did not even exist? Furthermore, we all depend on our brains and our cognitive faculties to form any kind of ideas, and there will never come a time when we will no longer be dependent or required to have faith in our cognitive faculties in order for us to even be able to function in any way, shape, or form.

The truth of the matter is, limited, finite beings with a beginning like us, or in other words everything besides God, have no choice but to have faith, and that is precisely what God asks us to do, He asks us to believe in Him, and have faith in Him because He is the only being who is Independent, and He is the only Eternal, who existed when nothing else did exist. And we have no knowledge except that which He has given us. He is the only being that is infinite and depends on no one else, whereas everything else depends upon Him.

At times in our ignorance, we demand that only when we see God, we would believe in Him. We fail to realise that we would still need faith, even if we were to see God! Besides, the sight of God is the biggest blessing one could possibly ever have. Not every wicked, arrogant, disbelieving person would ever get to taste this ultimate blessing. Those people who have faith, who do righteous deeds, and those who enter heaven by the grace of their Lord, would indeed one day get this honour to look at the face of their Lord.

Consequently, it is recorded in an authentic narration, that the Prophet Muhammad said, 'When the people of paradise enter paradise, Allah, may He be exalted will say, "Do you want anything more?" they will say, "Have you not made our faces bright? Have you not admitted us to paradise and saved us from hell?" Then the veil will be removed and there will not be anything more beloved to them than looking at their Lord, may He be glorified and exalted.'[22]

---

[22] Narrated by Tirmidhi.

In another narration, the Prophet was asked, 'Did you see your Lord?' He replied, 'Light, how could I see.'[23] Meaning, that Prophet Muhammad could not see Allah, but what he did see was the veil of Allah which is made of light. If this veil were to be lifted for us in this worldly life, it would burn and destroy everything, and the creation of Allah would not be able to stand its effect. It is only out of Allah's mercy that He would empower His faithful believers with the ability to set their eyes upon Him in the next life.

---

[23] Narrated by Muslim.

Beyond the Stars

Do you settle for this lowly life?
Of gold and glitter and some false pride?
'Cos for you awaits more than ever,
A life of eternal bliss you could imagine never!

You are much more than what you think!
This world and its everything is but just for a blink!
For your destination is much further and far,
For you awaits a world beyond the stars!

To reach that place no money avails,
No wealth, no power, no war or assails,
To claim that place the key is but one,
To believe and have faith in The Almighty, The One!

The faith that will give you a sight,
Make you see things clearer and bright,
The likes of which you would never see,
With all of the science and sophistry.

So give up your greed to blindly gather,
All that you see of money and matter,
For your destination is much further and far,
For you awaits a world beyond the stars!

Summary

Striving for this life and all the material wealth that it has to offer, and to assume that this is all that there is, could be the result of our ignorance and lack of our understanding of reality. Under the Islamic worldview, this is not all that there is to strive for. There is much more waiting for us in a life to come which we do not see for now. A whole new world in the afterlife which we could assure for ourselves if we channel our efforts in the right direction, have faith, work righteous deeds in the obedience of God, and in pursuit of His pleasure.

Science is a very essential and valuable tool today in the possession of mankind. It is a vital and important tool to know about this world that we live in, which never stops to bewilder and amaze us. It helps us to know more about ourselves and our surroundings and has helped and continues to do so to better our lives. But science, no matter how amazing and useful it is, has its own limitations. Science can never give us the absolute Truth with a capital 'T'. In this case, would it be wise to look for the Truth with a capital 'T' in science and reject other roots of knowledge like reason, logic, testimony, and most importantly revelation, which does claim to be the Truth from God, who has one of His attributes as *Al-Haqq* (The Truth) in Islam?

In order to find The Truth, we need to let go of our unfounded and unsubstantiated presuppositions, that the only way we can know about anything is through science. We need to give revelation a chance and see whether it can answer for us the questions that we long had, and long to know the answers of. And once we do so, it could completely change the way we look at things and give us a completely different and new perspective on life.

Gardens of Heaven

On couches reclining they will be,
Believers that day in the Most High,
Fruits from branches hanging in abundance,
In the gardens given by the Most High!

Rivers with clearest of waters,
No sun hot enough to hide,
Cool, gentle breezes of heaven,
Beautiful, chaste, ever-loving brides!

Carrying goblets of gold and silver,
Pass by boys of eternal youth,
Serving them drinks, finest of wines,
On their couches as they relax and recline.

Their dress they feel, soft and delicate,
Green, of rich silk with beautiful brocade,
Kings they are of all that is in sight,
No enemies to worry for, no enemies to fight!

No fatigue they feel, no worry, no grief,
No lies they hear, no falsehood, no deceit,
All that they say and hear is peace and peace,
To one another amongst them as they meet and greet.

This, for all the good works that they did,
Believing in their Lord, and the rewards that He promised,
So let those who work, work for such an end,
A well-pleased Lord, and the gardens of heaven!

Summary

The descriptions of paradise in this poem are taken from the Quran, largely from the seventy-sixth chapter. The Islamic literature is filled with descriptions of the paradise and events that are to take place in the hereafter. After all, is it not from the curiosity of man to know what is out there on the other side?

Is it all Real?

What is it all that I see?
The sounds I hear, the birds on the trees,
The rivers and oceans, mountains and seas,
And the breeze that flows gentle and free!

The sun up in the sky that brightens my day,
Until all darkness runs away,
The moon and the stars at night they stay,
Until the dawn of another new day.

The people I meet, the places I go,
The love I experience, the joy and sorrow,
Is it all real? I sometimes question,
Is there a meaning to my life from which I run?

No sense life makes without a meaning,
No difference remains between the dead and the living,
To give me my meaning to make me human,
There is only one being the Lord of the heavens!

Without whom there is no purpose there is no meaning,
Life void of which becomes unreal and unpleasing,
So let those who in their hearts lack content,
Acknowledge their Lord and the Prophet whom He sent!

Summary

The most rational conclusion that a person can come to when he observes the complex and intelligently designed realities that surround his life is to affirm a creative power behind it, which then helps to ascribe purpose and meaning to everything around him. Without a creator God, life, and everything that we see around us reduces to an unwanted, unintentional, and unnecessary accident. There remains no meaning to investigate the mysteries of life. There remains no reason to live life itself.

On the other hand, when a person affirms the existence of God, he can with confidence ascribe meaning to his life and all that surrounds his life. Once a person acknowledges the existence of God, and recognises the divine nature of the revelation, it not only becomes easy to understand this life, and ascribe meaning to it, belief in the aspects of the unseen, like the afterlife, which plays an important role in giving meaning to this present life that we live also becomes very easy, reasonable, and justifiable. And once a person does so and aligns himself with reality and remembers his Lord often, it is then that he feels contentment in the heart.

O My Heart!

O my heart! why do you make my life so difficult?
With thousands of desires piled one above the other,
What is it that you want from me?
Don't you see what harm you do to me?

You ask for things beyond my reach,
With all your tantrums and your deceit!
You make life difficult, unviable,
O my companion! untrustworthy, unreliable!

Why do you want that which is not yours?
Why not be content with all that is yours?
Why do you deem greener, the grass the other side?
How many nights for you have I cried?

O my heart! all your tantrums make a big mess,
Be a little grateful and show some thankfulness!
Surely I won't give you all that you need!
For I am a human, humble and weak!

There is a watcher who for me set some rules,
I won't obey you but follow His rules!
Who created you and placed you firm in my chest,
All your whispers and desires for me are a test!

And if I hearken and fall prey to your charms,
My life may swerve away from His commands,
Between you and Him it's Him that I choose,
My life and my death in His service must I use!

No man on earth can fulfil all your demands,
Nothing on earth can fill you up by any chance!
But yet there is something that will truly suffice you,
Put an end to all this trouble you do!

It is the dirt and the dust that will surely fill you,
When in my grave they lay me for a beginning new!

Summary

Prophet Muhammad, peace and blessings of God be upon him said, 'If the son of Adam were given a valley full of gold, he would love to have a second one, and if he were given the second one, he would love to have a third, for nothing fills the heart of Adam's son except dust.'[24]

There is no end to the desires that we have in this life. There is always going to be something in life that we will not have. Money could never possibly buy us anything and everything that we want, and it certainly can never buy us contentment and peace of the heart. The only place where our hearts could possibly find contentment and satisfaction in this life is in the remembrance of our creator.

---

[24] Narrated by Bukhari.

Tribulations Two

No man that walked the path of God but faced tribulations two,
The ones that troubled all of them seeking the path of truth.

The doubts that lurk and attack from within,
Until the believer questions his faith, his most beloved of all things!

The blameworthy desires then are not any less,
To swerve a believer from his path of success.

And together these two, doubts and the desires,
Led many a man astray, to the path of the fire!

So, let the believers beware!
Against these enemies two take every precaution and care.

As for the doubts repel it with knowledge,
Pray to the Lord to undo its damage.

Ask Him to protect and strengthen your heart,
Until all your worries from you begin to depart.

And think of your death to fight your unlawful desires,
The standing before your Lord, and the pit of the fire!

Summary

In the Islamic tradition, the two major and also the most dangerous tribulations of the heart are *shahawat* (blameworthy desires) and *shubuhat* (doubts about religion).

Islamic scholars argue that doubts are more dangerous than blameworthy desires. For doubts can lead a person outside the fold of Islam once he rejects any of the six pillars of faith or any fundamental aspect of religion due to these very destructive doubts. At times, doubts can resemble truth, though they are nothing more than falsehoods dressed up in the clothing of truth.

During the times that we live in, a systematic propaganda against Islam by some people in power is evident and clear for all to see. It is through such propaganda and probably other misleading sources a person may develop false notions or doubts regarding the clear teachings of Islam. Therefore, it is very vital to examine the source from which a person learns or takes information about Islam. Seeking knowledge from the right sources is probably the best strategy to fight these doubts.

And as for the blameworthy desires, the best strategy is to remember our finite nature and remember that surely there is going to come a day when we will be standing in front of our Lord, a day when He will question our actions and our misdeeds. A day when good actions will be rewarded, and sin and transgression will justly be punished. For our Lord who promised us to reward us when we do good in this life, also possesses equal right and power to punish us if we sin and transgress and reject His message when it reaches us for no good reason.

The Most Beloved Thing

I set out on a journey one fine day to find,
The most beloved thing of this world I hold in my mind,
To find it and cherish it as long as I live,
To give thanks to the Most High for the gift that He gives!

'Maybe it's my mother,' I said to myself,
Who gave me my birth and took my care more than herself,
Loved me the most without any doubt,
Told me often that of me she was so proud!

But how would my life be without a father?
Without my siblings, our fights and our laughter?
My spouse who loves me as much,
Or is it my son, or is it my daughter?

One by one I counted them all,
The things that I have and all I could recall,
The house that I lived in which gave me respite,
And the fleets of my vehicles ready for me to ride!

The food that I eat, and my farms where it grows,
The money, the gold, and the silver that I own,
The property that I amassed over the years,
With my blood, sweat and my tears!

I asked myself and everyone I knew,
In my hunt for this thing of the most value,
I looked down under and up above the skies,
To the north, to the south, between sunset and sunrise!

And thinking of my death, I soon realised,
Where this precious gem lay hidden from all eyes,
On my death, when everything will abandon me,
My friends, my well-wishers and my family!

When my wealth and my money would be of no avail,
From the unseen when that day will be lifted the veil,
On that day, my faith in God will never fail me,
To help me go through my new life ahead of me.

When the angels appear and begin to question,
'Who is your Lord?' Where would I run?
'Who was Muhammad, the one whom He sent?'
The life that He gave how did I spend?

O how I wish I be steadfast that day!
Make my faith stronger to God I pray!
Indeed it is my faith which I would cherish all my life,
That which would help me in my eternal new life!

Summary

The most valuable gift a person can possess in this life is faith. Because it is faith in God that makes human beings human. Without God, and faith in God it is impossible to distinguish between man and an animal and even man and inanimate object for that matter. Without faith in God, one gets reduced to mere atoms and molecules.

It is faith in God which helps a person to distinguish right from wrong. It is faith in God which gives a person a sound understanding of morality and ethics. It is faith in God which gives a person a reason to exist, and a purpose in life. It is faith in God which helps a person live a meaningful life. And it is through this faith in God, that we are promised salvation and an eternal life of bliss and joy in our afterlives.

The Prostration

Though it looks difficult at times,
You seem unsure about it at times,
But what harm can there be if you once try,
Who knows you could win if you just try?

And no matter what the world tells you about you,
Puts you down and talks ill about you,
Know that if you trust and believe in yourself,
No power on earth can hold from you, what you deserve for yourself!

And if you feel weak, and think that you need some help,
You are all alone on your own, no helper to help,
Know that you have Him by your side,
The creator of the heavens to help you and guide!

So stand firm, and hold to your grounds,
Believe in yourself, and to your problems never bow down,
Seek help and guidance from your Lord instead,
To Him draw closer, in prostration place your head!

Summary

Prophet Muhammad, may peace and blessings of God be upon him said, 'The nearest a servant comes to his Lord is when he is in prostration, so make supplication in this state.'[25]

No matter how wealthy and powerful a person becomes, there comes a situation in life when one realises that not everything is under one's control. No matter how hard one tries, one simply cannot change a certain situation or avert certain problems in one's life. So therefore, after one exerts all of one's efforts, to change a certain situation in life, and if it bears no results, one must know that there is always hope in God. For He can help us in ways and manners we would hardly ever understand. So therefore, we must put our trust in God and in our sincere efforts and be sure that one day our efforts will bear fruits.

---

[25] Narrated by Muslim.

The Last Bit

I hide my tears behind my eyes,
And all my fears beyond all eyes,
I am I think about to give up hope,
But this last bit in me just won't let it go!

And every time I am in my lowest of lows,
I refuse to give up, I refuse to bow,
However big my problems may be,
Through them this last bit makes me go!

'You will make it,' the sound in me says,
'Just don't give up,' over and over it relays,
'Get up from the misery and never lose hope,
Clinch a bit harder to God's divine rope!'

And at an instance I bow my head and prostrate,
To Allah I turn, worship and pray,
'O Allah, I am weak I am your slave,
Give me some strength and show me the way.

In distress I turn to you humble, repentant,
Of the sins I committed being so persistent,
Have mercy and forgive your repentant slave,
Before he ends up dead into his grave!'

And raising my head off the ground I feel,
Every wound that I ever had begins to heal,
Optimistic again I begin to feel,
Forgiveness of my Lord, and His love so real!

Summary

No matter how dark the night may be there is always hope for a new dawn. No matter how distant one might feel from God, all it takes is a few steps to reach God. No matter how many mistakes a person might have committed in life, there is always a way to rectify. A person should never give up, nor feel unworthy of God's love, for His divine mercy and love encompasses everything, and He accepts and forgives all those who turn to Him in repentance.

The Repentance

I took one step, or maybe two,
Towards the Almighty, the right thing to do,
And just as I began to draw a bit closer,
I sinned and slipped and felt like a loser!

I lay in defeat, losing all my hope,
Snapping from me His divine rope,
But before I quit, I once again tried,
Repenting from my sins, I begged Him and cried!

And soon I felt His grace and mercy again,
Away from me went all of my pain,
And just as I got up again to walk His way,
I slipped and sinned, falling even astray!

I am doomed I said, this is my end,
I am a hypocrite, I just pretend,
But before I give up, let me give it my all,
Seek His forgiveness, to Him let me call.

And the Oft-Forgiver indeed replied,
Forgave me my sins, to Him as I cried,
Showered His blessings all over again,
Away from me went all of my pain!

Striving in His path, I doubled my efforts,
Praised Him in my best, and even my worst,
And no sooner I thought I was in control,
I sinned and fell in even a bigger hole!

Covered in shame, full of regrets,
I couldn't believe how often I could forget,
I thought I might never make it,
No promise I make, except that I break it.

As hard as it felt, I rose up again,
To lose hope in Him was misguidance so plain,
I did it all over again what I had to do,
Took one step towards Him, or maybe two.

Summary

Repentance is a never-ending process. A person can never stop repenting for he can never stop sinning against God. Consequently, the Prophet of God, Muhammad, may peace and blessings of God be upon him said, 'All of the children of Adam are sinners, and the best of sinners are those who repent.'[26] In another narration he said, 'By Him in whose hands is my soul if you were not to commit sin, Allah would sweep you out of existence, and He would replace you by those people who would commit sin and seek forgiveness from Allah, and He would forgive them.'[27]

So those people who have committed sins in life should never lose hope in the forgiveness and mercy of God, for He forgives all sins. One should never ever feel unworthy of having a relationship with God because of the sins one has committed in life. For in fact one of the most beloved things to God is the repentance of His slave. The Prophet said, 'Allah is more pleased with the repentance of His believing servant than a person who loses his riding beast carrying his food and drink. He sleeps

---

[26] Narrated by Tirmidhi.
[27] Narrated by Muslim.

(being disappointed about its recovery) and then gets up and goes in search of that until he is stricken with thirst, then he comes back to the place where he had been before and goes to sleep again, completely exhausted, placing his head upon his hands, waiting for death. And then, when he wakes up this time, out of nowhere, there is before him his riding beast, his provisions of food and drink. Allah is more pleased with the repentance of His servant than this man and the recovery of his riding beast along with provisions of food and drink.'[28]

It is in the nature of human beings to be imperfect, to forget, to commit mistakes, and to advertently or inadvertently sin. But there is always hope. There is hope because the Lord who created human beings is the Most Forgiving and the Most Merciful. Consequently, God says in the Quran, **'Say, "O my servants who have transgressed against themselves, do not despair of the mercy of Allah. Indeed, Allah forgives all sins, indeed it is He who is Oft-Forgiving, the Most Merciful."'**[29]

In another place He says, **'Your Lord has written mercy for Himself, so that if any of you does evil in ignorance and thereafter repents and does righteous good deeds, then surely He is Oft-Forgiving, Most Merciful.'**[30]

---

[28] Narrated by Bukhari.
[29] The Quran, Chapter 39, Verse 53.
[30] The Quran, Chapter 6, Verse 54.

The scholars of Islam outline four steps for one's repentance to be accepted by God. The very first step is to acknowledge and accept one's wrongful actions as being wrong and a sin. The second step is to stop committing that wrongful action or sin. The third step is to firmly resolve not to repeat that sin in the future and sincerely ask God for His forgiveness. Finally, the last step is to try to undo the wrong that one did. For instance, if a person unlawfully got hold of someone else's property he should return it to the rightful owner, seeking the owner's forgiveness. These are the four steps of repentance that scholars of Islam mention.

Am I Free?

I sat one day to wonder,
Am I really free to do things right or to blunder,
Or is everything already determined,
To the laws of nature am I confined?

Being a believer that I am,
I asked for guidance from the God of Abraham,
'Cos the worms of philosophy were too much to handle,
The more I read, the more it all seemed but a scandal!

What law now can make me write what I write?
Million other things I could have done or just sat quiet,
Did He really plan everything for me?
Is it all His will or am I really free?

Clouds of my doubts began to depart,
As I remembered His verses in my heart,
That which said I can only will,
Until and unless it falls under His will!

Summary

The one thing that atheism and Islam agree upon is determinism, well at least to some extent. Determinists argue that everything that we see and observe in the universe is a result of a prior cause and that includes absolutely everything, including us and our actions. The actions that we do are a result of our genetics, our environment, and forces over which we have no control, it is either nature or nurture that we act upon. In other words, atheists believe, at least most of them, that the free will that we experience is nothing more than an illusion, and that ultimately, we are just puppets of nature. All our actions can be traced back into the past even before our birth and in the same way they could be predicted far into the future until our death and beyond. And there is a reason for atheists to be hard-core determinists. For under atheism, how could one possibly explain free will?

It is this free will that breaks every law of physics or nature one can possibly imagine. Imagine yourself jumping up for an instance. A scientist could very well explain how the food you ate broke down producing energy in your body, and how your leg muscles helped you overcome the pull of gravity for a few seconds, but what could possibly explain you jumping up at that particular point of time and not some other time? What can possibly explain why it is you who jumped up and not someone else?

There is a simple reason why atheists deny free will. It is simply because there is no answer for it in a Godless universe where all that there is, is blind forces interacting with one another producing varied results. If they were to acknowledge free will, it would be akin to opening the door to the unseen and the metaphysical and ultimately to God. It would be exceedingly difficult for them to acknowledge that it is not just biology and natural forces that drive the human body and its actions, it is something more than that, it is consciousness, it is a soul, and that in turn would require acknowledging the giver of this consciousness and the soul, someone beyond matter and material.

To avoid and deny this reality, most atheists stringently adhere to determinism and overlook and altogether reject the most obvious intuition of freedom we experience in our daily lives. If you still are a hard-core determinist, try jumping up and down for no reason and try finding the causal chain that led you to do so!

Adhering to this causal chain, however, has its own challenges. With the recent scientific developments, it is almost impossible to deny the fact that the universe began to exist at a certain point in time and that it does not go infinitely into the past. What cause can the determinist cite to explain the springing of the universe from nothing, for nothing has no potential to be identified as a cause for something i.e. the universe? Determinists at this point reach, to what I call the point of no return, on one hand, accepting free will leads to the opening of the door to divinity which they so fervently wish to close, on the other hand, determinism strips them of the most obvious of our feelings of freedom and free will and fails to explain and address the origin of the universe.

Islam tackles the issue of determinism very profoundly. In the Islamic worldview, everything that we see and observe and every event that takes place in this universe is the result of the 'first cause' i.e., God, and not just any random causal chain. This first cause, which is God, is the only eternal being who requires no further explanation or causes. This first cause is a personal being, with intention and will, because He chose to give rise to and initiate the universe which reflects that He has a will, and this God who possesses a will, perfectly explains the free will that we possess, which He endowed upon us.

One of the pillars of Islam is divine decree. All that has ever happened or will happen in the future, happens in accordance with the will of Allah. So where do we as humans stand in this picture? Are we really free in any way or is it all the will of Allah and are we just its manifestation? To better understand the concept of divine decree in Islam, let us consider an analogy.

Say a babysitter was hired to look after a six-year-old boy. The babysitter brings some of the toys the boy has, and asks if he would like to play, to which the boy agrees, the babysitter then sits himself down and watches the boy as he plays with his toys. Notice that in this scenario the boy's will and the will of the babysitter coexist and that there is perfect harmony and synchrony. The boy could have chosen not to play at all, but he did so out of his own free will, which happened to coincide with the will of the babysitter. Let us say in another scenario the boy prefers not to play with his toys which the babysitter brings out for him, he instead asks the babysitter to allow him to watch TV for some time, to which the babysitter agrees. In this case, the will of the boy and the babysitter initially were not in harmony, but the babysitter allowed the boy to go ahead and act upon his will. In the third scenario let us say the babysitter, instead of bringing the toys, brings some of the boy's books and asks him to finish his homework. The boy hates to study. He flatly refuses, but this time the babysitter insists, and the boy, though reluctantly and unwillingly, but yet in the end finds himself doing his homework.

In the first and second scenarios, the boy's actions were completely out of his own free will with the approval of the babysitter in both. In the last scenario, however, the boy was forced to study even though he never wanted to, and the boy acted completely in accordance with the will of the babysitter.

The analogy above aptly represents the free will that we possess, and the relationship that it has with the will of God. The free will that God endowed upon us is in no way absolute. It must always be approved by God, in other words, there is a limit to the free will that we have, and the limit is the will of God.

This is what is mentioned multiple times in the Quran, **'And you do not will except that Allah wills. Indeed, Allah is Ever-Knowing and Wise.'**[31]

Sometimes, what we will or intend to do is exactly what God desires and wills for us, so He allows us to go ahead and act upon our intentions. At times our actions, good or bad, are solely out of our own free will, which God approves for us, in His divine wisdom, and allows us to act. And there are other times, when our will is in conflict with the will of God, in this case, we fail to act or achieve our goals, however much we try. In any case, it is the will of Allah that prevails, and this does not take anything away from the fact that we too possess a free will, but it is just that it is not absolute, it has a limit, and the limit of our free will is the will of Allah. It must at all times pass through the will of Allah.

---

[31] The Quran, Chapter 76, Verse 30.

Secrets of a Happy Life

Secrets of a happy life are two,
The one that helps one go through,
The ups and downs of one's way,
Keeps one happy and all of one's worries at bay!

First is to know that there is a divine,
To know that it is all His not mine,
To have faith in Him with all of one's heart,
To fulfil one's duties to Him, and to do one's part.

The other is to have in Him one's reliance,
Trust all His plans and to them be compliant,
Never to His decree ever object,
Accept all His decisions with utmost respect.

Together these qualities two,
Of faith and reliance help one in life go through,
Until a person begins to embrace,
One's joy and one's sorrow, all with His praise!

Summary

Strong faith in God coupled with faith in the divine decree of God can work wonders to change an individual's perspective on life. No matter how much people try to harm you, they can only harm you as much as God wills. The situations whether good or bad that you go through in life are all through the will of God. Your job is to be the best possible person you could be in any given situation. This faith in God coupled with faith in God's divine decree puts a person's heart at complete ease, no matter how favourable or difficult the situation might be. Consequently, Ibn Abbas reported, 'I was behind the Messenger of Allah, peace and blessings of God be upon him when he said to me; "Young man I will teach you some words. Be mindful of Allah and you will find Him before you, if you ask, ask from Allah, if you seek help, seek help from Allah, know that if the nations gather together to benefit you, they will not benefit you unless Allah has decreed it for you. And if the nations gather together to harm you, they will not harm you unless Allah has decreed it for you. The pens have been lifted and the pages have dried."'[32]

---

[32] Narrated by Tirmidhi.

One Step at a Time

My heart runs ahead of me,
It has so much it wants from me,
Many an unfinished work which remain,
Many a place to go after this rain.

It runs yet ahead of me,
As if it will from me almost flee,
More it wants, even if a few,
Something a little different, something a little new.

Calm down a little, O my companion!
On this old friend you have some compassion!
Take it easy, give it some time,
Take a small step, one at a time!

I know it's new and maybe it's true,
A new path to life, I never knew,
But take it easy, give it some time,
Take a small step, one at a time!

*I know it's exciting I know it's new,
I know maybe the right thing to do,
But take it easy, it will just be fine,
Take a small step, one at a time.*

Summary

At times it can be almost overwhelming to try new things. But this is not the right justification to altogether refuse to experience new opportunities and new paths that life may offer, as this may hinder an individual's growth and progress. Instead of getting stressed up about all the changes one might have to undergo while taking a new path, one must concentrate on at least moving towards this new path, even if it means taking little baby steps towards it.

Miles Away

I said my prayers, and did some good,
I went for Hajj,[33] and fasted too,
Helped the hungry, fed them food,
Gave my time, and all I could!

Helped my neighbours, and the orphans too,
The sick, the blind, and the destitute,
By the poor and oppressed, I often stood,
In the path of God, I did all good.

The more I do, the more I say,
My goal from me, is yet miles away,
The good I do, must never stop,
My goal from me, is yet miles away!

---

[33] *Hajj* is the annual Islamic pilgrimage, and fifth pillar of Islam. The other four pillars are the *Shahada* (declaration of faith), *Salat* (five daily prayers), *Sawm* (fasting of *Ramadan*), *and Zakat* (annual charity).

Through the work I do, I only seek,
The face of Allah, The Almighty,
I must go on, and never give up,
The good I do, must never stop!

The more I do, the more I say,
My goal from me, is yet miles away,
The good I do, must never stop,
For my goal from me, is yet miles away!

Summary

We must never stop our good works and continue on our path to God seeking His pleasure. His pleasure should be our only motivation for our good works. The work that we do in His path should not be our only focus and our end destination but rather our focus and end destination should be His pleasure and countenance. The good work that we do for the sake of Allah is but a means to get closer to Allah and seek His pleasure and not the end.

Conclusion

Do not just yet give up on life. There are answers to the questions of life. We need to look for them in the right place.

Ever since man set foot on this earth, Almighty God kept sending His prophets and messengers to guide us and show us what He wants from us. This prophethood ended a little more than fourteen hundred years ago upon Muhammad, may peace and blessings of God be upon him. Consequently, God placed this responsibility of sharing His message upon the followers of Muhammad.

God may He be glorified said in the Quran, **'You are the best nation brought out for mankind, commanding what is righteous and forbidding what is wrong.'**[34]

No prophet of God would ever come to warn mankind ever again. For God said, **'Muhammad is not the father of any of you men, but the Messenger of Allah and the seal of prophets. Allah has full knowledge of all things.'**[35]

God gave His final message to mankind in the Quran. We therefore must try to understand His message

---

[34] The Quran, Chapter 3, Verse 110.
[35] The Quran, Chapter 33, Verse 40.

and try to live our lives in accordance with His final message which has for over fourteen hundred years been preserved in the Quran. The earlier messages that the prophets brought from God, they all have been changed and most of them have even been lost. The only message that remained preserved for over a thousand years is that of the Quran and in extension of Islam. Not because the message was different, for it was the same message that all the prophets before Muhammed came with. It was preserved like none of the earlier messages precisely because there will not be any new messages coming from God until the end of times. Therefore, God glorified be He, took it upon Himself to preserve His last message. Consequently, He said, **'It is We who have sent down the Quran, and surely We will guard it from corruption.'**[36]

Life sans God becomes meaningless, without a purpose for our existence. All our actions and our deeds get reduced to meaningless trivialities. A person might adopt atheism without getting exposed to the true message of God, and once he does so, his life ends up with all sorts of difficulties and problems and all sorts of unanswered questions one could imagine. There remains no reason to be morally upright, for there remain no morals and no values. There simply remains no reason to live life, which often leads to depression and anxiety.

On the other hand, when a person acknowledges the reality, and acknowledges God, his heart and mind

---

[36] The Quran, Chapter 15, Verse 9.

find contentment and peace. His life becomes meaningful, and he gets a joy out of life which he could never get no matter where he were to look for it in life.

If you feel convinced of the existence of God, and if you believe in the prophethood of Muhammad, these are considerably the two basic conditions for a person to enter the fold of Islam. If you need any kind of assistance in your journey to *Islam*, the Arabic word which simply means submitting oneself to the will of God, which one can do by accepting the divine guidance given in His final revelation, or if you need to declare your *shahada*, or if you have some reservations and doubts regarding Islam, please visit your nearest Islamic centre for help.

And lastly, if you think you benefited from this book and its message in any way, shape, or form, make sure that you become a part of this good cause of spreading this message of God, by promoting this book and its message, and helping as many people as you can in their journey to find God and the answers to the mysteries of life.

About the Author

The author, Muneeb Ahmed Qazi, is a graduate in Education and in Engineering. He has always had a passion for writing, and this is his first-ever book that he has authored. You can contact him to share your valuable comments or feedback at-

qazimuneeb1994@gmail.com

Alternatively, you can follow him on X (previously known as twitter) using the handle-

@muneebqazi94.

Made in the USA
Columbia, SC
12 January 2025